# War, Peace, and All That Jazz
## 1918–1945

## TEACHING GUIDE
## FOR THE 3RD EDITION

OXFORD
UNIVERSITY PRESS

Oxford University Press

Auckland   Bangkok   Buenos Aires   Cape Town
Chennai   Dar es Salaam   Delhi   Hong Kong   Istanbul   Karachi
Kolkata   Kuala Lumpur   Madrid   Melbourne   Mexico City   Mumbai
Nairobi   São Paulo   Shanghai   Singapore   Taipei   Tokyo   Toronto

And an associated company in Berlin

Published by Oxford University Press, Inc.
198 Madison Avenue, New York, New York 10016

Writers: Chip Brady and Phil Roden, Deborah Parks, Karen Edwards
Editors: Robert Weisser, Susan Moger
Editorial Consultant: Susan Buckley

ISBN 978-0-19-976743-4

Printed in the United States on acid-free paper

# CONTENTS

# NOTE FROM THE AUTHOR

*Dear Teacher,*

It is through story that people have traditionally passed on their ideas, their values, and their heritage. In recent years, however, we have come to think of stories as the property of the youngest of our children. How foolish of us. The rejection of story has made history seem dull. It has turned it into a litany of facts and dates. Stories make the past understandable (as well as enjoyable). Stories tell us who we are and where we've been. Without knowledge of our past, we can't make sense of the present.

As a former teacher, I knew of the need for a narrative history for young people, so I sat down and wrote one. (It took me seven years.) I was tired of seeing children struggle with arm-breaking, expensive books. I wanted my books to be inexpensive, light in weight, and user-friendly. Thanks to creative partnering by American Historical Publications and Oxford University Press, that's the way they are.

Called *A History of US,* mine is a set of 11 books. My hope is that they will help make American history—our story—a favorite subject again. It is important that it be so. As we prepare for the 21st century, we are becoming an increasingly diverse people. While we need to celebrate and enjoy that diversity, we also need to find solid ground to stand on together. Our history can provide that commonality. We are a nation built on ideas, on great documents, on individual achievement—and none of that is the property of any one group of us. Harriet Tubman, Abraham Lincoln, Emily Dickinson, Sequoya, and Duke Ellington belong to all of us—and so do our horse thieves, slave owners, and robber barons. We need to consider them all.

Now, to be specific, what do I intend these books to do in your classrooms? First of all, I want to help turn your students into avid readers. I want them to understand that nonfiction can be as exciting as fiction. (Besides, it is the kind of reading they'll meet most in the adult world.) I want to stretch their minds. I've written stories, but the stories are true stories. In nonfiction you grapple with the real world. I want to help children understand how fascinating that process can be.

I've tried to design books that I would have liked as a teacher—books that are flexible, easy-to-read, challenging, and idea-centered, that will lead children into energetic discussions. History can do that. It involves issues we still argue about. It gives us material with which to make judgments. It allows for comparisons. It hones the mind.

People all over this globe are dying—literally—because they want to live under a democracy. We've got the world's model and most of us don't understand or appreciate it. I want to help children learn about their country so they will be intelligent citizens. I want them to understand the heritage that they share with all the diverse people who are us—the citizens of the United States.

For some of your students, these books may be an introduction to history. What they actually remember will be up to you. Books can inspire and excite, but understanding big ideas and remembering details takes some reinforced learning. You'll find many suggestions for that in this Teaching Guide.

What you do with *A History of Us* and this Teaching Guide will depend, of course, on you and your class. You may have students read every chapter or only some chapters, many volumes or only a few. (But, naturally, I hope they'll read it all. Our history makes good reading.) I hope you'll use the books to teach reading and thinking skills as well as history and geography. We need to stop thinking of subjects as separate from each other. We talk about integrating the curriculum; we need to really do it. History, broadly, is the story of a culture—and that embraces art, music, science, mathematics, and literature. (You'll find some of all of those in these books.)

Reading *A History of Us* is easy; even young children seem to enjoy it. But some of the concepts in the books are not easy. They can be challenging to adults, which means that the volumes can be read on several levels. The idea is to get students excited by history and stretched mentally—at whatever their level of understanding. (Don't worry if every student doesn't understand every word. We adults don't expect that of our reading; we should allow for the same variety of comprehension among student readers.)

This Teaching Guide is filled with ideas meant to take the students back to the text to do a careful, searching read. It will also send them out to do research and writing and discovering on their own. The more you involve your students, the more they will understand and retain. Confucius, one of the worlds' great teachers, had this to say:

*Tell me and I will forget. Show me and I will remember. Involve me and I will understand.*

History is about discovering. It is a voyage that you and your students can embark on together. I wish you good sailing.

Joy Hakim with two of her favorite readers, her grandchildren, Natalie and Sam Johnson

*Joy Hakim*

# ABOUT THIS TEACHING GUIDE

Like *A History of US*, this Teaching Guide is designed as a flexible resource to be used with students at varying levels. The guide for each volume presents conceptual frameworks, teaching strategies, and assessment suggestions as well as a range of activities for enrichment and extension.

## Teaching with Big Ideas

The themes that run through human experience help us organize ideas and understand events. They enable all of us—and especially young students of history—to make sense of the stories of the past. Book Nine deals with four Big Ideas: **political systems, justice, conflict,** and **change**. They provide the conceptual framework that holds together the 44 chapters and hundreds of individual stories in this volume of *A History of US*.

## Creating Teaching Units

We have divided each volume of *A History of US* into Parts, or units of study, whose chapters have a common theme or focus. The Teaching Guide is organized to help you create a unit of study around each Part:

> **Part 1: Uncertain Peace (Chapters 1-3)**
> **Part 2: Normalcy? (Chapters 4-8)**
> **Part 3: An Age of Heroes (Chapters 9-14)**
> **Part 4: Boom and Bust (Chapters 15-18)**
> **Part 5: Rendezvous with Destiny (Chapters 19-25)**
> **Part 6: The World in Flames (Chapters 26-32)**
> **Part 7: Turning the Tide (Chapters 33-38)**
> **Part 8: Redefining War and Peace (Chapters 39-45)**

## Special Features

**Literacy and *A History of US*** describes the strategies for literacy instruction that are integrated throughout the Teaching Guides and are further developed in the *Literacy Handbook for Reading History*.

**About the Johns Hopkins Team Learning Activities** introduces the teaching materials developed by the Talent Development Middle School project at Johns Hopkins University. Selected lessons appear in these Teaching Guides.

**Assessment and *A History of US*** outlines strategies and instruments for assessment in the Teaching Guides and Assessment Package.

**Historical Overview** presents the broad historical context for the stories and ideas in this volume of *A History of US*.

# Teaching Strategies

**Introducing Book Nine** includes suggestions for presenting the book's conceptual underpinnings, strategies for a focus on literacy, and descriptions of ongoing projects.

**The Introduction** to each Part links the content with the Big Ideas, sets goals for teaching, and sets a context for reading as well as for studying geography and chronology.

**Chapter Lesson Plans** for each chapter have a three-part organization:

- Connect
- Understand
- Check Understanding

**Marginal Notes** include suggestions for Reading Nonfiction, Geography Connections, Linking Disciplines, and Meeting Individual Needs, and provide background information and links to the *Sourcebook* for *A History of US*. Information about additional resources, such as web sites, may also be found here.

**A Johns Hopkins Team Learning Activity** is included after the Chapter Lesson Plans for each Part. These activities provide opportunities for students to work in groups for collaborative learning.

**The Summary** for each Part presents suggestions for Assessing the Part, Debating the Issues, Making Ethical Judgments, and Projects and Activities.

# Synthesizing the Big Ideas

A series of questions—which you can use for assessment or discussion—provides opportunities for students to deepen their understanding of the Big Ideas as they relate to the events, trends, and personalities presented in the volume.

# Part Check-Ups and Resource Pages

At the end of this teaching guide are pages that can be reproduced for student consumption, including Check-Ups for each Part, outline maps, primary sources, and enrichment material.

# LITERACY AND
# *A HISTORY OF US*

*In our Information Age, reading is an essential survival skill. So what does this have to do with us historians and history educators? We have the key to the nation's reading crisis, and we've been ignoring it: When it comes to critical reading, history shines. Hardly anything approaches it in its demands for analysis and thinking.*

Joy Hakim

Teaching with *A History of US* gives you a special opportunity to focus on literacy. As Joy Hakim notes, "Nonfiction is the literary form of our time." As highly readable nonfiction, *A History of US* can be a tool for teaching strategic reading skills.

## Literacy Skills in the Teaching Guides

**Strategies for Reading Nonfiction** appear in the margins of chapter lesson plans. Each strategy is designed to facilitate the development of nonfiction reading skills linked to specific aspects of the chapter. Strategies are organized into the following categories:

- *Analyzing Text Organization:* Strategies to guide student analysis of the writer's purpose in using structures such as compare/contrast, cause and effect, proposition and support, sequencing, and so on

- *Analyzing Text Features:* Strategies to guide student analysis of features such as text format, sidebar material, and captions

- *Analyzing Point of View:* Strategies to develop student ability to identify and analyze expressions of an author's voice and opinions

- *Analyzing Graphic Aids:* Strategies to help students analyze information presented in maps, illustrations, photographs, charts, and other graphic material

- *Analyzing Rhetorical Devices:* Strategies to help students identify and analyze rhetorical devices such as author questions and persuasion

- *Analyzing Primary and Secondary Sources:* Strategies to guide students in differentiating between and comparing primary and secondary sources within the text, as well as analyzing author's purpose for their selection

- *Analyzing Word Choice:* Strategies to focus student attention on the message, method, and effect of specific vocabulary such as expressions, descriptive words, signal words, and figurative language

**Strategies for Reading Comprehension** are integrated into the suggested classroom instruction in the Book, Part, and Chapter teaching strategies. These include *Setting a Context for Reading* in the Book and Part Introductions and *Thinking About the Chapter* in the Chapter lessons. Skills include the following:

- Sequencing
- Identifying Cause and Effect
- Making Comparisons
- Contrasting
- Identifying Main Idea
- Summarizing
- Generalizing
- Predicting
- Making Inferences
- Drawing Conclusions
- Identifying Point of View

## Literacy Handbook for Reading History

The *Literacy Handbook for Reading History*—a publication to accompany *A History of US*—guides and enriches instruction in literacy skills for reading history. Focusing on the particular skills and techniques for reading history, the handbook presents strategies that apply to all nonfiction reading.

In its introduction, the *Literacy Handbook for Reading History* links literacy and history, differentiates between learning to read and reading to learn, and guides you in introducing students to the individual elements of reading the ten volumes of *A History of US*.

The heart of the handbook organizes strategic reading into Before Reading, During Reading, and After Reading steps.

Reproducible pages include graphic organizers, worksheets for teaching comprehension skills, and worksheets for analyzing documents and other text features. Pages can be used to create transparencies and/or student handouts.

# USING THE JOHNS HOPKINS TEAM LEARNING ACTIVITIES

**JOHNS HOPKINS**
U N I V E R S I T Y

The Talent Development Middle School Program at Johns Hopkins University is a project of the Center for the Social Organization of Schools (CSOS). *A History of US* is the core of the American history curriculum in this whole-school reform effort. Oxford University Press proudly includes in this Teaching Guide selected lessons developed by Susan Dangel and Maria Gariott at the Talent Development Middle School Program.

You will find one Johns Hopkins Team Learning Activity at the end of each Part in this Teaching Guide. Keyed to appropriate chapters, the Team Learning Activity provides an opportunity to use cooperative learning models based on *A History of US*.

Each Activity begins with a *Focus Activity* that introduces the lesson, engages students, and draws on students' prior knowledge.

The heart of the lesson is a *Team Learning Activity*. In teams, students investigate lesson content, solve problems, use information for a purpose, and apply the tools of the historian.

Within the Student Team Learning Activity, the following techniques and strategies may be employed:

- *Brainstorming:* Students generate as many ideas as possible within a set time, before discussing and evaluating them.

- *Roundtable:* A brainstorming technique in which each team member contributes ideas on one sheet of paper and passes it to the next student. In *Simultaneous Roundtable*, more than one sheet is passed at the same time.

- *Round Robin:* An oral form of brainstorming in which one team member at a time states an idea.

- *Think-Pair-Share:* Students think about content or consider a question, then share their responses with a partner. In *Think-Team-Share*, students think through the prompt on their own and then share as a team.

- *Partner Read:* Students share a reading assignment with a partner.

- *Timed Telling:* A student or team is given a fixed time to share information, opinions, or results with the class.

- *Team Investigation:* Working in teams, students search and analyze the text, primary source materials, or other resource materials; draw conclusions; and make connections.

- *Jigsaw:* Within each team, students select or are assigned specific questions or subjects on which to become experts. Experts meet and investigate in Expert Teams, then regroup in their original teams to report out their findings.

- *Numbered Heads:* Each team member is assigned a number—1, 2, 3, and so on. Team members work together on the team learning activity. The teacher selects one number and asks the person with that number in each team to report the team response.

Author Joy Hakim intentionally omits from her books the kinds of section, chapter, and unit questions that are used to review and assess learning in standard textbooks. It is her purpose to engage readers in learning—and loving—history. Rather than interrupting student reading, all assessment instruments for *A History of US* have been placed in the Teaching Guides and in the Assessment Package.

# ASSESSMENT AND
# *A HISTORY OF US*

## In the Teaching Guides

**Ongoing Projects** are set up with assessment guidelines in the Introduction to each book.

**Check Understanding** sections in each chapter lesson plan provide a *Writing* assignment that checks student understanding of chapter content. *Thinking About the Chapter* suggestions, based on thinking skills, assess student ability to interpret chapter content and concepts.

**Synthesizing the Big Ideas** at the end of each Teaching Guide uses essay questions to pull together major concepts and themes.

**Part Check-Up** pages provide study guides that review content and Big Ideas for each Part. (These blackline masters appear at the end of each Teaching Guide.) In addition, *Alternate Assessment* suggestions at the end of each Part ask students to make connections with Big Ideas across chapters.

## In the Assessment Package

Recognizing educators' need to prepare students for standards-based assessment, Oxford University Press has prepared a separate Assessment Package to accompany *A History of US*. Included in the Assessment Package are

- rubrics for evaluating writing assignments in the Teaching Guides.
- machine-scoreable tests to assess learning in each Part.

# HISTORICAL OVERVIEW

The "Big Four" at Versailles peace conference

Babe Ruth

Bessie Smith, jazz singer

*The faith of Americans in their own country is religious, if not in its intensity, at any rate in its almost absolute and universal authority....Our country is still figured in the imagination of its citizens as the land of promise. They still believe that somehow and sometime something better will happen to good Americans than has happened...in any other country; and this belief, vague, innocent, and unformed though it be, is the expression of an essential...national ideal.*

In his 1909 classic of Progressive literature, *The Promise of America,* Herbert David Croly proclaimed optimism as a national ideal. He eagerly awaited future progress. But the future also held some of the greatest challenges since the Civil War—challenges that would test American optimism.

One of the most serious challenges came in 1914, when years of imperialism and nationalism catapulted Europe into war. Despite a strong isolationist voice within the United States, German aggressions at sea pulled the nation into the war on the side of the Allies.

Upon entering the conflict in 1917, President Woodrow Wilson, champion of American idealism, promised to make the world "safe for democracy." When the guns fell silent in 1918, Wilson championed an ambitious peace plan called the Fourteen Points. After the destruction of war, however, few Allies shared Wilson's thirst for a "peace with honor." The Senate went even further and refused to ratify the Versailles Treaty because of disagreement over the League of Nations. "I can predict with absolute certainty," warned an embittered Wilson, "that within another generation there will be another world war if the nations of the world do not...[find] the method by which to prevent it."

In 1920, however, few Americans heeded Wilson's warning. They felt that the nation had done its part in preserving democracy. They wanted to forget about war and get on with their lives. Republican candidate Warren G. Harding understood this and promised "normalcy," a return to past values and practices. Americans elected Harding by a landslide.

The 1920s belonged to the Republicans. The party weathered the scandal-filled Harding era to usher Calvin ("Silent Cal") Coolidge into the White House. Coolidge believed in "less government in business and more business in government." The policy seemed to work. For much of the 1920s, the economy boomed, and many urban Americans enjoyed an unprecedented prosperity.

Below the bubbly optimism of the 1920s, however, trouble was brewing. Prejudice reared its ugly head in the form of the Red Scare and restrictions on all immigration into the United States. Overproduction of farm products produced surpluses and declining prices. Membership in hate groups rose, while union membership dropped. Meanwhile, a heady buy-now-pay-later attitude led people to spend beyond their means.

On Black Tuesday, October 29, 1929, disaster struck. Stock prices plummeted in a massive wave of selling, and the market crashed. Just seven months before, president-elect Herbert Hoover had declared, "I have no fears for the future of our country. It is bright with promise." As the stock market crash spread into a more generalized economic depression, many Americans despaired. Within a year, millions of Americans were jobless, bankrupt, or both. Unlike earlier depressions, this one wasn't about to turn around soon.

The American economy hit rock bottom in 1932. That year, optimism reappeared in the form of an exuberant New York Democrat named Franklin Delano Roosevelt (FDR). In a whirlwind campaign, Roosevelt pledged "a new deal for the American people." Desperate for change, voters swept Roosevelt into office. During his first 100 days, FDR pushed through a massive package aimed at achieving the three R's: *recovery* from the Depression, *relief* for victims of the Depression, and *reform* of the nation's economic system. More important, he rekindled hope.

As the 1940s opened, FDR had more to worry about than the economy. Throughout Europe and Asia, democracy faltered under the heavy hand of totalitarian rulers, and a second World War began. Isolationists again tried to shield the United States from the conflict. But a Japanese attack on U.S. ships at Pearl Harbor in Hawaii proved that the United States could no longer insulate itself from the affairs of the world. On December 8, 1941, the United States entered World War II.

For the second time in 25 years, the United States mobilized to defend world democracy. This time, however, the nation fought a two-front war. Battles in the Pacific cost Japanese Americans their rights as the government questioned their loyalty and herded them into internment camps. Despite this injustice, many Nisei enlisted in the war. So did some 15 million other American men and women. Their efforts—and new weaponry—turned the tide in the Allied favor.

In 1945, on the eve of Allied victory, FDR died after serving only three months of his unprecedented fourth term. Ending the war now fell to Harry Truman. Fascist Italy collapsed first, then Nazi Germany. Japan's warlords refused to surrender. Only after U.S. planes dropped atomic bombs on Hiroshima and Nagasaki did Japan surrender.

Book Nine traces the path from the failure of the League of Nations to the rise of the United Nations. Each of the eight parts recommended for teaching this book serves as a "roadmarker" on this journey.

**Part 1: Uncertain Peace    1914-1918**
**Part 2: Normalcy?    1917-1927**
**Part 3: An Age of Heroes    1914-1931**
**Part 4: Boom and Bust    1928-1932**
**Part 5: Rendezvous with Destiny    1920-1933**
**Part 6: The World in Flames    1933-1941**
**Part 7: Turning the Tide    1941-1945**
**Part 8: Redefining War and Peace    1945**

War is over!

# TEACHING STRATEGIES FOR BOOK NINE

## INTRODUCING
*BOOK NINE*

# Introducing the Big Ideas

**B**ook Nine deals with four Big Ideas: **political systems, justice, conflict,** and **change.** They provide the conceptual framework that holds together the 44 chapters and hundreds of stories in this volume of *A History of US.*

You might introduce the concept of political systems by reading the quote by Franklin Roosevelt on page 8 (facing the Preface). What do students think he means when he says that Americans are the authors of the "living book of democracy"?

Next, introduce students to the ideas of justice and conflict by asking how democratic and non-democratic governments differ in their view of justice. Ask students what happens when nations disagree over the definition of *justice. (Conflict erupts.)* Now have students skim the Table of Contents. Do they think World War I resolved conflicts between political systems? Why or why not? *(No; a second world war erupted.)*

Reread the closing sentence of the FDR quote. Then ask students to preview the photos in Book Nine. Do students think the American people wrote "a story of retreat" or "a story of continued advance" during the years between the end of World War I (1918) and the end of World War II (1945)?

*NOTE FROM THE AUTHOR*

*How about testing? How will children do if they study these books? The old books focus on narrow, easy-to-memorize test questions. When children meet new questions, they are lost. This program challenges children to question, to develop their minds, to do research and writing, to think for themselves—as well as to learn specifics about the past. That is exactly what the SAT and the new tests look for.*

# Focusing on Literacy

## Setting the Context

To illustrate the changes that have taken place since the founding of our nation, assign students to read the Preface on pages 9-12. (You might select "storytellers" to take turns reading paragraphs aloud.) Encourage students to discuss the questions the author raises, as a class or in small groups. When students have finished, ask them to summarize changes that took place in our political system between 1789 and today. Would the founders say our society had become more just? Why or why not?

## Charting Cause and Effect

You might begin the book by reviewing the definitions of *immediate cause* and *underlying cause* and *short-term effect* and *long-term effect.* Then set up large sheets of paper on which students can create ongoing and changing diagrams of the causes and effects of the Great Depression and World War II.

## Reading Further

You may wish to have partners read biographies of such people as FDR, Eleanor Roosevelt, Harry Truman, Marion Anderson, Duke Ellington, Joseph Stalin, Adolf Hitler, Dwight Eisenhower, and Douglas MacArthur, and then present short oral reports to the class.

## Ongoing Projects

The following activities bridge the eight parts in Book Nine.

*I recommend Kieran Egan's book* Imagination and Learning *(University of Chicago Press). Egan writes of the importance of imagination and creativity in developing intellect. Writing stories from history demands organizational skills; it forces you to make choices; it makes you think. Have your students try writing their own stories.*

## Using Time Lines

Students can create class and personal time lines that focus on the main block of time covered in Book Nine (1917-1945). The time lines can help students to identify the causes of two pivotal eras covered in this book—the Great Depression and World War II. The time lines can also show important effects of these events, especially their connection to what Joy Hakim calls the growth of big government.

**Assessment/Sequencing** When students have completed the class and/or individual time lines, organize them into small groups. Assign each group a period covered in Book Nine. Direct them to review the class and individual time lines, as well as the Chronology on pages 198-199. Then hand out note cards or sheets of paper and tell each group to draw pictures or write quotations or newspaper headlines for five events that took place during their period. When students are done, collect the cards or papers, shuffle them, and redistribute them, challenging each group to sequence the cards correctly.

## Using Maps

Several activities will enrich students' understanding of World War I and World War II. They will need a map of the world to show alliances, changes in alliances, and events. By mapping and color-coding the complex details of this period, they can visually organize the large picture.

**Assessment/Analyzing Maps** When students have completed their maps, ask: In which parts of the world was each country fighting? Were other countries fighting on two fronts?

## Writing History

The author hopes that students will become historians in their own way. She encourages them to retell and add to the stories in each book in *A History of US*. One way to accomplish this is to ask students to set up a separate section in their notebooks or in a three-ring binder in which they write their own history books. When you finish each chapter, give students time to write their own accounts of events.

**Assessment/Editing Historical Writing** When students have completed their own history books for Book Nine, have them exchange books with other students. Challenge students to pick one or two chapters in their classmate's book for editing.

## Teaching History

Assign teams of students to work cooperatively to teach portions of the book. Encourage them to enrich instruction with pictures, poems, art, and so on. The "teachers" should also devise short homework assignments or in-class activities. At the end of the lesson, the class should submit several questions to be used as part of a self-evaluation test.

**Assessment/Self-Analysis** If students have acted as teachers for the class, ask them to evaluate their own techniques.

# The Big Ideas

From 1914 to 1918, the conflict that people of the time called the Great War (World War I) shook the world. Although the United States didn't enter the war until 1917, its brief participation in that struggle would set off changes in the nation for many years to come. The end of the war was the real beginning of a new century, but few people could guess what that century would bring. An American woman who lived in France during the war captured the uncertainty many of her fellow citizens felt at the war's end. Just before the fighting stopped, she wrote the following lines:

*Yet out there I knew the guns were still firing. Between them and me lay such devastation as even the imagination cannot exaggerate, and such suffering and pain as human Teaching can but partly understand. Four years and four months— and how much is still before us? The future has its job laid out for it. Are ordinary humans capable of handling it?*

After the Great War ended, many Americans wanted to isolate themselves from the rest of the world. Others believed that lasting peace could come only by working with other nations.

# Introducing Part 1

## Setting Goals

Introduce Part 1 by writing its title, "Uncertain Peace," on the chalkboard. Discuss ways in which a peacetime or a peace agreement might be "uncertain." Refer to the title of Chapter 1, "War's End," and ask what war this refers to. *(World War I, then called the Great War)*

To set goals for Part 1, tell students that they will
- describe Woodrow Wilson's post-war goals and decide if any were achieved.
- analyze the points of view of American isolationists and leaders of other countries who had fought in the war.
- depict the effects of the influenza pandemic and the methods used to fight it.

## Setting a Context for Reading

**Thinking About the Big Ideas**    Ask students to suggest ways in which they think America had to change in order to fight in World War I. *(Possible responses: had to raise an army; had to produce more military goods; had to find new workers to replace those who left to fight)* Then ask students to think about what happened after the war. What changes were needed then? *(Possible responses: needed to reduce the size of the armed forces; needed to shift away from military production)* How might the changes after the war have led to conflicts in the society? *(Possible responses: People who fought in the war might have wanted their old jobs back, while those who took those jobs during the war might not have wanted to give them up.)* Tell students to look for other examples of conflict growing out of change as they read Part 1.

# PART 1

# Uncertain Peace

## [CHAPTERS 1-3]

**Analyzing Character**   Encourage students to analyze the characters of the people they meet in Part 1 and to note their strengths and their faults and how character affected their endeavors. For example, Woodrow Wilson had a strong moral righteousness, but he failed to include others in his planning and thus did not achieve most of his Fourteen Points and failed to get the United States to join the League of Nations.

## Setting a Context in Space and Time

**Using Maps**   Post for classroom display an up-to-date map showing the same area depicted in the maps on page 17 of Book Nine, and distribute the outline map of Europe, Resource Page 1 (TG page 102). Have students use the upper map in the book to label places in one color and the lower map to label them in another color. Ask how World War I changed the map of Europe. *(New nations appeared: Finland, Estonia, Latvia, Lithuania, Poland, Czechoslovakia, Austria, Hungary, Yugoslavia, U.S.S.R.)* Ask students if they think—based on the evidence of the maps—that World War I resolved many issues.

**Understanding Change Over Time**   Tell students that the three chapters of Part 1 deal with events that took place in just four years, 1914-1918. Have students flip through the pages of these chapters, looking at maps, photographs, and headings. Then refer them to the Chronology on page 200. Finally, direct them, based on their review of the chapters and Chronology, to complete this sentence: "The years from 1914 to 1918 were a period of _____." Have students save their sentences so the accuracy of their predictions can be checked when Part 1 is completed.

# War's End

[PAGES 13-15]

**1 Class Period**

## Chapter Summary

Under President Wilson's leadership, the United States joined the Allies in 1917 against the Central Powers in the Great War. In a remarkably brief time, many of the nation's factories converted from peacetime to wartime output, and millions of civilians became soldiers. U.S. contributions helped bring about Allied victory in November 1918.

## Key Vocabulary

Central Powers     neutral
Allies     armistice

## 1. Connect

Ask students to imagine the continuous noise of guns and other weapons. Then have them imagine that all the noise stopped at once. Point out that the noise—and the war—ended at a specific time—11 A.M. on the 11th day of the 11th month. Discuss how people might have felt when the Great War ended.

## 2. Understand

1. Read up through Wilson's words. Discuss: What important event took place on November 11, 1918? (*The Great War ended.*) What did President Wilson want after the war? (*the establishment of democracy throughout the world*)
2. Read the rest of the chapter. Discuss: Which countries formed the Central Powers? (*Germany, Austria-Hungary, the Ottoman Empire*) Which countries formed the Allies? (*Britain, France, Russia, Japan, Italy, and the United States*) What events led to America's entry into the war? (*Germans sank neutral American ships because they believed the United States couldn't prepare quickly for war.*)

## 3. Check Understanding

**Writing**   Ask students to write a paragraph explaining why the author says President Wilson was strong.

**Thinking About the Chapter (Analyzing)**   Engage students in a discussion about why special war powers allowed President Wilson to prepare the nation quickly for war. (*The nation would be able to prepare to fight more rapidly if the President didn't have to have Congress debate each need.*)

## Note to the Teacher

When you see the instruction "Read…," you can interpret it in any way that fits the lesson you are creating for your students. For example, you may read aloud to the class or to small groups, you may have volunteers read aloud, or you may have the class read silently.

## Reading Nonfiction

*Analyzing Primary and Secondary Sources*

Ask students to locate the text features that include primary sources and to read them. What conclusions can they draw about how people viewed the end of the Great War? (*People were relieved and optimistic about the future.*) Then have students read the author's last paragraph on page 15. What does the author imply by saying "or so it seemed"? (*She implies that the people's optimism was going to be short-lived.*)

## Meeting Individual Needs

Have students who are visual learners compare the photos on page 13 with those on pages 14 and 15 to learn about the war. (*The lower photo on page 13 shows a sad scene of soldiers carrying the wounded. The photos on pages 14 and 15 show celebrations.*)

## History Archives

*A History of US Sourcebook*
#73, Woodrow Wilson, *War Message* (1917)

## Reading Nonfiction

*Analyzing Text Features*

Have students read the feature on page 20. Ask students to think about why the author presents this information about the Espionage and Sedition acts in a sidebar. (The information is important and interesting; the acts were passed in response to the war, but the acts are not a main point of the chapter.) Ask how students would answer the author's questions in the second paragraph.

## Geography Connections

Distribute Resource Page 1 (TG page 102). Have students study the maps on page 17 and also the world map in the Atlas. Ask them to identify countries that weren't independent before the war ended and mark them on their outline maps. Have students circle countries that have changed since then. (*Finland, Estonia, Latvia, Lithuania, Poland, Czechoslovakia, Austria, Hungary, Yugoslavia, Turkey, Syria, Iraq, Palestine, Transjordan*) Discuss the fact that most of these are still independent countries today.

## History Archives

*A History of US Sourcebook*

#74, Woodrow Wilson, *"The Fourteen Points"*: *Address to Congress* (1918)

## Activities/Johns Hopkins Team Learning

See the Student Team Learning Activity on TG page 22.

# Fourteen Points

[ PAGES 16-20 ]

**1 Class Period**

## Chapter Summary

President Wilson hoped that the victorious Allies would offer the defeated Central Powers a generous treaty that would ensure a lasting peace. His hopes were dashed, however, both by the harsh terms of the final treaty presented at Versailles and by the refusal of the U.S. Senate to take part in the League of Nations, a new world organization.

## Key Vocabulary

League of Nations     sedition
self-determination     espionage

## 1. Connect

The Great War had ended, and now it was time to make a great peace. Ask students to recall Wilson's hopes for "the establishment of a just democracy throughout the world" and have a student read aloud the margin quote on page 16. How do would Wilson try to achieve democracy in the world? Would he succeed?

## 2. Understand

1. Read through the end of the first paragraph on page 18. Discuss: What points of view did Wilson fail to understand in suggesting a generous peace? (*After a long difficult war, the winners wanted to punish the other side. People, especially leaders, don't like others to tell them what to do.*)
2. Read the rest of the chapter. Discuss: How did the treaty deal with Germany? (*It was blamed for the war and had to pay war costs.*) What happened to the League of Nations? (*The U.S. Senate would not pass the treaty to authorize the United States to join the League.*)

## 3. Check Understanding

**Writing** Ask students to read the quote from Clemenceau in the margin on page 16. Have them write a paragraph that gives an opinion about the question: If President Wilson had seven points instead of fourteen, would it have made a difference?

**Thinking About the Chapter (Analyzing)** Ask students to explain reasons that the United States did not join the League of Nations. (*Some Americans wanted to stay out of Europe's problems; Senate Republicans hoped opposition to the League would help them win the next election.*)

# Another Kind of War

[ P A G E S   2 1 - 2 4 ]

**1 Class Period**

## Chapter Summary

As World War I wound down, Americans and people around the world found themselves fighting another deadly enemy. This enemy was a strain of influenza (flu) that would kill millions of people around the world.

## Key Vocabulary

| | | |
|---|---|---|
| influenza | pandemic | normalcy |
| epidemic | swine flu | |

## 1. Connect

Have students name diseases against which people today are vaccinated. (*for example, measles and whooping cough*) Ask: Do you know anyone who gets flu shots? Tell the class that none of these vaccinations and medicines existed in 1918. Point out to students that people today are faced with a similar situation regarding HIV-AIDS, a disease that kills people around the world and for which we do not yet have a vaccine.

## 2. Understand

1. Read through "…wiped out" on page 23. Discuss: Which killed more people, the war or influenza? (*Influenza killed 10 times as many people.*) What did people do to try to prevent influenza? (*They wore gauze masks, which had little effect.*)
2. Read the remainder of the chapter. Discuss: What did Americans long for? (*normalcy*) What were two issues Americans discussed after the war? (*doing away with liquor and equal rights for women*)

## 3. Check Understanding

**Writing**   Tell students to imagine that they are living in Chicago during the 1918 influenza outbreak. Have them write letters to friends or relatives in other cities describing the impact of the disease.

**Thinking About the Chapter (Comparing and Contrasting)**
Some people compare the influenza pandemic to the AIDS epidemic of today. Have students compare and contrast the two health care crises. (*Possible similarities are that they spread without any medical ability to cure them. Possible differences are that we have some ideas of prevention and some ability to control the fatality rate of AIDS and that we are not arresting people who do not follow the rules.*)

## Linking Disciplines

*Art/History*

Point out that many people today are accustomed to styles of art like the painting on page 24, but in 1913, it was totally new. Discuss the public reaction to the art style in 1913.

## More About...

*Marcel Duchamp*

When Marcel Duchamp sent *Nude Descending a Staircase* to a gallery in Paris in 1912, the gallery refused to hang it. In New York a year later, this painting shocked the public more than other paintings in the show. Duchamp gave up painting shortly after the 1913 Armory show.

## 1 Class Period

### Focus Activity

**1.** Have volunteers read aloud the Beverly Cleary quote in the feature on page 15. Remind students that Beverly Cleary wrote many children's novels, such as the *Ramona* series, *Dear Mr. Henshaw*, and *Henry and Beezus*. Discuss why Beverly's mother might have wanted to impress the importance of the day on her daughter.

**2.** Ask students to describe how they might feel or react when a war ended. What would affect their reactions and the reactions of their families? (*Reactions would depend on whether a person or family had been directly affected by the war.*)

### Student Team Learning Activity/Evaluating Main Ideas

**1.** Have Students **Partner Read** Chapter 2. Then divide the class into teams to analyze the "Fourteen Points" speech (in *A History of US Sourcebook*) and discuss information in Chapter 2 relating to the Fourteen Points.

**2.** Write the following questions on chart paper or the chalkboard. Have students use **Think-Team-Share** to answer them. Each student should be prepared to share with the class his or her team's responses.
- How do these terms relate to Wilson's Fourteen Points: *isolationism, self-determination, Treaty of Versailles, League of Nations*?
- As a team, decide which five or six points of the Fourteen Points are the most important. Explain each of your choices.
- What went wrong? Why didn't Wilson get his just peace? List all the factors that defeated Wilson's peace plans.
- Wilson considered the League of Nations the most important of his Fourteen Points. Do you agree? Why or why not? Connect your argument to a present-day world organization and its role in enforcing world peace.

**3. Circulate and Monitor** Visit each team to assist students with the readings and discussion of the questions. Encourage oral elaboration, ask and answer questions, and check that answers are accurate and supported by information from the readings.

**4. Sharing Information** Have students use **Numbered Heads** to share their responses to the questions. As needed, add information from the Overview, the Preface, and Chapters 1 and 2. Help students clarify the main ideas.

# Summarizing Part 1

## Assessing Part 1
**Part 1 Check-Up**    Use Check-Up 1 (TG page 94) to assess student learning in Part 1.

## Alternate Assessment
Have students write an essay answering the following question that links the big ideas across chapters:

**Making Connections**    What was the link among World War I, the influenza pandemic, and the growing desire for normalcy in the United States? (*Students should cite the enormous dislocation and changes brought on by the world conflict and the outbreak of disease, both of which fueled the desire of many Americans to return to what they thought of as simpler times before the war—normalcy.*)

## Debating the Issues
Use the topic below to stimulate debate.

**Resolved**    That the United States should join the League of Nations. (Suggest to students that they think of this as a U.S. Senate debate after the war, and that some students express the views of Wilson and the Democrats while others represent the role of Lodge and the Republicans.)

## Making Ethical Judgments
The following activity asks students to consider issues of ethics.

Free speech is one of the major guarantees of the Bill of Rights. Yet in Chapter 2, the author describes how some anarchists were jailed for exercising that right. The majority of the Supreme Court upheld their convictions. Review details of the case on page 20, and then explain how you would have voted had you been a member of the Court.

## Projects and Activities
**Designing a Front Page**    Challenge students to create the front page of a U.S. newspaper that might have carried news of the World War I armistice. Remind them that their front page should carry at least one headline, illustration, and story.

**Composing a Speech**    Have students write a speech that Woodrow Wilson might have delivered to a French audience urging adoption of his Fourteen Points as part of any peace treaty.

**Using Historical Imagination**    Ask students to imagine they are medical students at a women's medical school or a black medical school and have read Abraham Flexner's report, mentioned on page 23. What would they suggest as an alternative to closing down their medical school? How would they support their suggestions?

## Looking Ahead
*Making Predictions*

After the war, many Americans longed for a return to normalcy. But there were already signs of more trouble ahead. A British visitor to America in 1919 described some of these signs:

*I saw a luxury of wealth in New York and other cities which may be a vicious cancer in the soul of the people. I saw a sullen discontent among wage earners and homecoming soldiers because too many people had an unfair share of wealth....I heard of anarchy being whispered...in American cities....And now and then I was conscious of an intolerance of free thought which happened to conflict with popular sentiment....I saw hatred based on ignorance and the brute spirit of men inflamed by war.*

Tell students as they read Parts 2, 3, and 4 to look for evidence that supports or refutes these signs of trouble in the United States.

# PART 2

## Normalcy?

### [CHAPTERS 4-8]

## The Big Ideas

Changes had swept through the nation during World War I. More changes loomed ahead in the 1920s. How did the American people want their government and its leaders to deal with those changes? During the 1920 presidential race, Republican candidate Warren G. Harding said that he and his party would bring:

*Not heroism but healing, not nostrums [quack cures] but normalcy, not revolution but restoration, not agitation but adjustment, not surgery but serenity...not experiment but equipoise [evenness and balance]....*

Harding and normalcy won in a landslide. Part 2 describes the strains created as the American political system attempted to cope with an era of rapid changes.

## Introducing Part 2

### Setting Goals

Introduce Part 2 by asking, "What exactly is normalcy?" Ask students to recall some of the changes that had taken place after World War I. How would different parts of the U.S. political system respond to the changes that shook American life after World War I?

To set goals for Part 2, tell students that they will
- consider the change brought about by Prohibition and its unanticipated consequences.
- describe the new rights women had at the ballot box.
- characterize the nature of the federal government under Harding and Coolidge.

### Setting a Context for Reading

**Thinking About the Big Ideas**   Tell students that Calvin Coolidge (who served as president for much of the 1920s) once said, "Four-fifths of all our troubles in this life would disappear if we would only sit down and keep still." Ask students whether they agree with Coolidge. Do they think that this advice applies to how government operates? Tell students to keep these points in mind as they read about a decade in which nothing ever seemed to keep still.

**Drawing Inferences from Pictures**   Ask students to leaf through the pictures in Chapters 4-8. Discuss how these images tell a story on their own, apart from the written words. Ask students what they can infer from the various illustrations. (*Students can infer the interest in prohibition and its effects, the active and successful movement for women's suffrage, the fear of anarchy and the rise of hate, and scandals in one president's term and the new social movements taking place—including the increase in automobiles.*)

## Setting a Context in Space and Time

**Using Maps**  Display a wall map of the United States or refer students to the Atlas. Tell students that with the admission of Arizona and New Mexico in 1912, the nation had assumed the physical shape and size it would hold for the next 47 years, until the admission of Alaska and Hawaii.

**Understanding Change Over Time**  Remind students that ten-year periods are known as decades. Point out that people often group historical events by decades as a way of getting a better grasp of complex events. Then read aloud the following list of labels that have been applied to the 1920s: *the Roaring Twenties, the Golden Twenties, the Jazz Age, the Aspirin Age, the Age of Wonderful Nonsense.* Ask what each of these labels suggests about the character of the 1920s. Tell students to keep the labels in mind as they read Parts 2 and 3.

## Reading Nonfiction

*Analyzing Vocabulary*

Have students go through Chapter 4 to identify words that came about because of Prohibition. Encourage students to explain how words like bootlegger, rumrunner, speakeasy, and other terms were coined. Ask students if they can think of any words related to events or customs of today.

## Linking Disciplines

*History/Art*

Point out that three illustrations in this chapter are paintings by Ben Shahn, a well-known artist who often painted subjects relevant to his time. Ask students to suggest subjects they might want to paint to illustrate events or social issues today.

## Meeting Individual Needs

Help ESL students read the feature on page 27. Work with students to distinguish between a law and an amendment. Point out that an amendment becomes part of the Constitution itself; that is, it becomes part of the basic law of the nation. A law, on the other hand, can be passed or changed more easily. Ask students to explain in their own words the difference.

# The Prohibition Amendment

[ P A G E S 2 5 - 2 8 ]

### 1 Class Period

### Chapter Summary

In time, a well-intentioned desire to eliminate alcohol abuse in the United States produced two constitutional amendments and a wide variety of unexpected, unintended consequences.

### Key Vocabulary

| | | |
|---|---|---|
| prohibition | per capita | bootlegger |
| rumrunner | speakeasy | |

## 1. Connect

Remind students that returning soldiers found many Americans at home were determined to end the drinking of alcohol. Ask students what they think might happen if alcohol were made illegal today.

## 2. Understand

1. Read pages 25-27 through "All but two states passed the Prohibition Amendment." Discuss: Why did many people in the United States favor Prohibition? *(Many believed drunkenness led men to waste their paychecks and leave their families without money and drinking was also harmful to the drinker.)*
2. Read the rest of the chapter. Discuss: What unexpected effects did Prohibition have? *(Some people who had not drunk before started to drink because it was fashionable. Gangsters took over the sale of liquor and crime became a big business.)*

## 3. Check Understanding

**Writing**  Ask students to create two lists, the first giving reasons for Prohibition, the second giving reasons to end Prohibition.

**Thinking About the Chapter (Making Ethical Judgments)** Engage the class in a discussion of whether alcohol should have been made illegal. Encourage students to give their opinions on whether the lessons of Prohibition apply to illegal drugs as well. *(Students will have differing opinions. They may recognize the role crime plays in drug traffic, but they may also cite the deadly effects of some drugs.)*

# Mom, Did You Vote?

[PAGES 29-33]

## 1 Class Period

## Chapter Summary
In 1919, ratification of the 19th Amendment, guaranteeing women the right to vote, marked a major milestone in the long battle for women's rights.

## Key Vocabulary
suffrage          suffragist

## 1. Connect

Remind students that the second issue that returning soldiers encountered was women's demands for equal rights. Ask students if this was a new issue. (*Students should recall women's rights issues from the second half of the 19th century.*) Encourage students to find reasons the country may have been ready to begin accepting equal rights at this time.

## 2. Understand

1. Read pages 29-30. Discuss: Why were the women picketing at the White House in 1917? (*They wanted President Wilson to support an amendment that would give women the vote.*) Were their activities illegal? (*yes*) Why were they arrested? (*Students may consider this in the light of other violations of the Bill of Rights they have already encountered. One possible answer is that leaders wanted to keep the status quo.*)
2. Read the rest of the chapter. Discuss: How did American women finally get the right to vote, and in what year did it happen? (*The 19th Amendment gave women the right to vote, and it was ratified in 1919.*)
3. Flowchart: Have students complete Resource Page 2 (TG page 103) to analyze the events involved in getting the 19th Amendment ratified.

## 3. Check Understanding

**Writing** Ask students to read "Female Takeover" on page 33 and then write a paragraph about how using the right to vote makes a difference.

**Thinking About the Chapter (Evaluating)** Encourage students to read the arguments for and against giving women the right to vote. Ask: which would have persuaded you and why?

## Reading Nonfiction

*Analyzing Word Choice*

After students read the poem on page 33, ask them to identify the words Miller uses to show a gradual change in "Mr. Jones's" point of view over a six-year period. (*subject, submit, glum, pride, etc.*) Then ask them to analyze Carrie Catt's quote in the caption on page 33. Which word signals a generalization? (*The word "no" in "no woman faltered."*) Discuss that Catt's statement is an example of the bandwagon technique of persuasive speech—she implies that all the women "joined the crowd" or joined "the winning side."

## Geography Connections

On a large map of the United States, have students locate San Francisco and Washington, D.C. Distribute Resource Page 3 (TG page 104) and ask students to identify some of the major geographical features the motorcade had to cross. (*Examples: Sierra Nevada, Great Basin, Colorado Plateau, Great Plains, Mississippi River, Appalachian Mountains*)

## Activities/Johns Hopkins Team Learning

See the Student Team Learning Activity on TG page 31.

## Reading Nonfiction

*Analyzing Point of View*

Have partners list words and phrases that help them understand the author's point of view toward anarchism and/or communism. (*"that sounds noble," "you don't have to be very smart,"* etc.) Then have partners write a sentence or two explaining the author's point of view toward these ideas.

## Meeting Individual Needs

Select advanced students to explain the ideas in this chapter to students who may need extra help interpreting the information.

# Red Scare

[ PAGES 34-36 ]

## 1 Class Period

### Chapter Summary

A fear of communism spread in the United States after the Russian Revolution of 1917, leading to the Red Scare, in which the rights of thousands of people were violated.

### Key Vocabulary

| | | |
|---|---|---|
| communism | reds | tsar |
| alien | anarchist | sedition |

## 1. Connect

Ask students what they know of communism. Read aloud the feature on page 34. Ask students to describe the events in Russia. Why were people in the United States worried about the communist revolution in Russia? (*As transportation and communication brought the world's people closer together, Americans worried about the spread of ideas they didn't like.*)

## 2. Understand

1. Read pages 34-35 through "but not in the history books." Discuss: Why were people in the United States worried about communism? (*They feared that communists would try to take over the country.*) What is an anarchist? (*An anarchist is a person who doesn't believe in governments and wants to do away with all governments.*) Could an anarchist be a communist? (*no*)
2. Read the rest of the chapter. Engage the class in a discussion about the rights people have in America. Discuss some of the rights that Mitchell Palmer violated. (*the right to have a warrant for arrest, to make a phone call, to have a trial to determine guilt*)

## 3. Check Understanding

**Writing**   Ask students to write a letter to the editor protesting the actions of Attorney General Palmer and basing their objections on their understanding of the Bill of Rights.

**Thinking About the Chapter (Analyzing)**   Read the Thomas Jefferson quote and the question presented by the author in the last paragraph of Chapter 6. Ask students to answer the question, citing evidence from Chapter 6 and knowledge of current events to support their point of view.

# Soft-Hearted Harding

[PAGES 37-40]

**1 Class Period**

## Chapter Summary
Although he was immensely popular, President Harding lacked the skills and abilities to meet the demands of the job. He died in office as scandal swirled around many of his friends and political appointees.

## Key Vocabulary
black migration

## 1. Connect

Explain that Woodrow Wilson's term as president was over, and the new president was Warren G. Harding. The war was also over, and the nation was looking forward to normalcy.

## 2. Understand

1. Read pages 37-38 up to "Warren Harding was one of the most popular presidents ever." Discuss: What are some qualities of a good president? (*hard worker, ability to pick good people for the administration, good communicator, good policies*) Does having these qualities ensure that a president will be popular? (*Students should express their views.*)
2. Read the rest of the chapter. Discuss: How did scandal mar Harding's administration? (*His friends and appointees had stolen natural resources and taken bribes from businesses and criminals.*)
3. Read and discuss the feature on page 40. Why did millions of blacks leave the South between 1910 and 1930? (*to find better jobs, schools, and homes in the cities of the North and Midwest*)

## 3. Check Understanding

**Writing**  Ask students to write a job description of the qualities they would like to see in a president.

**Thinking About the Chapter (Comparing and Contrasting)**
Read aloud the quotation that President Harding read from the book of Micah. Ask students whether the president lived up to the qualities in the quote. (*He had appointed friends that didn't do justice or love mercy, but he had also reduced the debt and appointed black men to office. Nevertheless, he left an administration that didn't live up to what he announced.*)

## Reading Nonfiction

*Analyzing Text Organization*

Have students reread the first three paragraphs on page 37 and identify the text structure the author uses. (*compare and contrast*) After reading the chapter, ask partners to make a Venn diagram to compare and contrast the physical features, accomplishments, and public perceptions of Presidents Harding and Wilson.

## Meeting Individual Needs

Encourage visual learners to examine the three cartoons in this chapter and tell how the artists got their messages across within a small space.

Read the feature Monkeys on Trial on pages 44-45. On the chalkboard, create two column headings using the quoted phrase from the 1st Amendment (page 45) ("Congress shall make no law respecting an establishment...") and the quoted phrase from the Tennessee law (page 44) ("unlawful for any teacher..."). Ask students to explain the points of view of each side in the Scopes trial in relation to these quotes. List students' responses on the chart.

# Silent Cal and the Roaring Twenties
[PAGES 41-46]

**1 Class Period**

## Chapter Summary
Sober, stolid Calvin Coolidge presided as president for much of the 1920s, a period in which the nation experienced both an economic boom and fast-paced social change.

## Key Vocabulary
| | | |
|---|---|---|
| Roaring Twenties | Jazz Age | flapper |
| monkey trial | evolution | Harlem Renaissance |

## 1. Connect

Remind students that Harding died in office in 1923, and Calvin Coolidge, his vice president, became president. Tell students that Coolidge was elected president in his own right in 1924 and served until 1929.

## 2. Understand

1. Read through "...and moved frantically" on page 43. Discuss: What were some changes that shook American society during the 1920s? (*Women's skirts and hair were worn shorter; there was a dance craze, the pace of life was faster, an increase in prosperity.*)
2. Read through "And these are just a few of the names" on page 46. Discuss: What problems seemed to go unnoticed? (*more people unemployed, many farmers in financial trouble*)
3. Read the last two paragraphs of page 46. Define *renaissance* as a rebirth and ask students to describe the phenomenon called the Harlem Renaissance. (*It was an explosion of artistic creativity in the 1920s by African Americans who had settled in the New York neighborhood of Harlem.*)

## 3. Check Understanding

**Writing**   Ask students to write the first paragraph of an article titled, "What Is a Flapper?"

**Thinking About the Chapter (Summarizing)**   Engage the class in a discussion of what made the Roaring Twenties roar. Discuss major changes that were taking place in America and ask students to suggest how people might have reacted to them.

# JOHNS HOPKINS
# TEAM LEARNING

## Taking a Stand on Women's Suffrage

## 1 Class Period

### Focus Activity

**1.** Have students generate a class list of words and phrases they associate with voting. (*election, poll, duty, privilege, apathy, right*)

**2.** Then ask them to list reasons why an 18-year-old might not be allowed to vote. (*criminal record or in jail, not a U.S. citizen*) Ask: Should the voting law be changed to allow more people, including teenagers under 18, to vote?

### Student Team Learning Activity/Identifying Point of View

**1.** Divide the class into teams and explain this simulation activity: The year is 1917. Your team is a civic group with a strong position for or against women having the right to vote. You receive a letter inviting representatives from your group to meet with other groups to argue your positions. Each member of your group will join a roundtable composed of members of other civic groups. Each person at the roundtable will have one minute to convince the others of his or her position. Remind students that women as well as men opposed women's suffrage and that men as well as women supported it.

**2.** Explain that each member of the team will be arguing the group's position to a different round table. This means the team must research and prepare a statement with strong arguments to support its viewpoint.

**3.** Assign each team a name from the following list: National Association for Woman Suffrage, Men and Women United for Woman Suffrage, Universal Suffrage Association, Woman Suffrage Movement, Americans Against Woman Suffrage, National Movement Opposing Woman Suffrage, Citizens Opposed to Woman Suffrage, Anti-Woman Suffrage Association. Make sure each team knows if it is for or against women's suffrage. Have each team member write the name of the group on a note card and provide yarn so they can wear the identifying cards around their necks. (*Note:* Have students within each team use different color inks to write the name of the organization on their card. The round tables will be color-coded so that all students whose group name is written in red will meet together; all whose cards are written in green will meet together, etc.)

**4.** Ask teams to Read Chapter 5 to find support for their group's position.

**5. Circulate and Monitor** Visit each team as students prepare their positions and one-minute speeches. As soon as groups are prepared (approximately 25 minutes), the representatives meet with their round tables. There should be four or five roundtables in your classroom.

**6.** Welcome the civic group representatives to the conference and remind them that each person on the roundtable has one minute to introduce the group he or she represents and then to present the group's position on women's suffrage. Use a timer to limit each presentation. If time permits, after all presentations open the floor to a general discussion within the roundtables.

**7. Circulate and Monitor** As the presentations are made, visit each round table to listen to the positions and arguments, and, if necessary to keep students on task.

**8.** Ask teams to **Think-Team-Share** answers to these questions: Did representatives from other groups change your position on the right of women to vote? Why or why not?

# Summarizing Part 2

## Assessing Part 2

**Part 2 Check-Up**   Use Check-Up 2 (TG page 95) to assess student learning in Part 2.

## Alternate Assessment

Ask students to design a graphic presentation of at least four main ideas from Part 2. Their graphics should have captions that explain the ideas.

**1. Making Connections**   What Constitutional amendment deals with issues raised by the Red Scare and the Scopes trial? *(The Red Scare raised issues connected with the First Amendment clause about freedom of speech; the Scopes trial involved the First Amendment issue of establishment of religion.)*

**2. Making Connections**   What was the connection between the Prohibition Era and the new styles in society? *(Prohibition made drinking more popular among some groups, especially young women; they flouted other customs by wearing short skirts, short hair, and makeup.)*

## Debating the Issues

Use the topics below to stimulate debate.

**1. Resolved**   That the U.S. government should take swift and stern action against communists and anarchists. (To encourage discussion, you might assign students some of the following roles: Attorney General A. Mitchell Palmer and his staff, immigrants who believe in communism, lawyers for the American Civil Liberties Union, members of the Ku Klux Klan.)

**2. Resolved**   That evolution should be taught in public schools. (Assign students to play the roles of John Scopes, Clarence Darrow, and William Jennings Bryan, as well as a university science professor and a fundamentalist Christian.)

## Making Ethical Judgments

The following activities ask students to consider issues of ethics.

**1.** Chapter 4 notes how Prohibition failed. The author then asks: "But how do you get people to stop doing something that isn't good for them? Do the lessons of Prohibition apply to drugs?...What do you think?" (Ask students to suggest other areas in which the government has moved to stop people from doing things that aren't good for them—anti-smoking laws—or to make people do things that are good for them—laws requiring seatbelts to be worn in cars or helmets for skateboarders, bicyclists, skaters, and other wheeled vehicles. Hold a classroom debate over one of these issues to highlight the clash between individual freedoms and the interests of the larger society.)

**2.** In Chapter 8, the author notes that the Supreme Court found state laws requiring the teaching of creationism to be unconstitutional because they conflict with the First Amendment guarantee of religious freedom. She then asks, "Do you understand why? Do you believe that guarantee to be important?" (Help students realize that separation of church and state continues to be a major issue today. Ask students to suggest recent cases on the subject, such as school prayer, displays of religious symbols in public buildings at Christmas time, etc.)

## Projects and Activities

**Writing an Editorial**   Have students review Chapter 4. Then divide the class into two groups. Have one group write editorials about the Prohibition amendment that would have appeared before the measure was ratified. Have the second group write editorials evaluating Prohibition's effectiveness several years after the amendment had taken effect.

**Designing a Poster**   Have students study the photograph on page 30 of suffragists at the White House. Then challenge students to design and draw other posters that suffragists might have carried at the White House or at other rallies supporting women's right to vote.

**Drawing a Political Cartoon**   Direct students to review the political cartoons in Chapter 6. Then have them create their own cartoons about some aspect of the Red Scare.

**Reading Aloud**   Select a student to read aloud to the class the quotation from Anne Martin, on page 29. Ask the class to consider whether similar petitions might be used by other groups to gain other rights.

**Using Historical Imagination**   Ask students to imagine they lived in the 1920s. What issues would have been important to them? How would their lifestyles have been different from or similar to those of their parents?

**Developing an Argument**   Read aloud the words of Dr. W. W. Parker on page 29:

> [Women are] superior morally, inferior mentally, to man—not qualified for medicine or law....God having finished this splendid world, placed at its grand arched gateway imperial man, stately and stalwart, with will and wisdom stamped upon his lofty brow.

Encourage students to use evidence from both the 1920s and today to develop an argument on this issue.

**Interpreting a Work of Art**   Refer students to the painting by Ben Shahn reproduced on page 28. Ask them to describe what they see. Who is shown in the painting? (*a bartender and fashionably dressed men and women*) What are they doing? (*They are in a speakeasy and are drinking.*) Does the place look disreputable? (*Most people would say no.*) How would you describe the mood and manner of the people?

## Looking Ahead
*Making Predictions*

Tell students that early in the 1930s an American writer looked back at how changes of the 1920s affected the nation and its people. He said:

> Americans...feel an uneasy, increasing sense of insecurity in the modern world, where they seem more and more to be the puppets of great economic forces which are beyond anyone's power to control. In this predicament they turn with relief to anyone who, in any field, appears to stand out beyond everyone else. They feel that the world needs giants—as perhaps it does.

Ask students to think about what they've learned about the 1920s thus far and then predict where Americans of the time might have looked to find "giants." Tell students to keep their predictions in mind as they read Part 3.

# PART 3

## An Age of Heroes

### [CHAPTERS 9-14]

## The Big Ideas

In the United States in the 1920s, change was occurring in all aspects of daily life. Growing use of the automobile brought change in where people lived and how they got to work. The growth of huge modern industries continued to change how people worked. Movies and radio were changing the way people got their news and the way they entertained themselves. In these years, even the heroes Americans looked up to and admired were changing. A writer of the time described this change:

> Hero-worship is not a new phenomenon in American life. But like many other things nowadays, it is speeded up and achieved on a larger scale....What we have seen in recent years is the creation of a vast new machinery for making everyone aware of any new person or idea....Let anyone say or do anything interesting, and within a week everyone in America has heard his voice on the radio, seen his photograph and read his interviews in the newspapers, seen and heard him in the movies.

In Part 3, readers will meet some of the "interesting" people of the 1920s who found themselves featured in the "machinery" of newspapers, movies, and radio.

## Introducing Part 3

### Setting Goals

Introduce Part 3 by asking students to look at the photos in Chapters 9-14. Do students recognize any of the people shown? If so, who? Encourage a discussion of why some heroes from the past remain heroes today.

To set goals for Part 3, tell students that they will
- identify the areas of endeavor that created heroes.
- describe the changes taking place in America that were part of what made them heroes.
- consider why some people who contributed to change are better known today than others.

### Setting a Context for Reading

**Thinking About the Big Ideas**    Read the following definition aloud to students or write it on the chalkboard: "someone admired for bravery, great deeds, or noble qualities or for contributions to a particular field." Ask students to suggest a word that fits this definition. (*hero*) Do they agree with the definition, or would they suggest any changes? Write down the revised definition if there is one. Point out that a nation's heroes can also change over time. Tell students as they read Part 3 to think about why some of the people discussed in it became heroes to Americans of the 1920s and why some remain heroes today.

**Making Predictions**    Ask students to predict areas of life that would produce some of America's heroes during the 1920s.

Write the areas students suggest on the chalkboard. After the class completes Part 3, have them examine the areas they identified and confirm or revise their predictions.

## Setting a Context in Space and Time

**Thinking About Geographic Concepts**   Remind students that from its beginnings, the United States had been a rural nation. Most people lived on farms or in small villages. On the eve of the Civil War, only 20 percent of the population lived in urban areas.

But industrialization was changing that pattern. By the beginning of the 20th century, about 40 percent of Americans lived in urban areas. Then, the 1920 census revealed that the figure had reached 51 percent. For the first time, more Americans lived in urban areas than in rural areas.

Ask students to suggest how this change from rural to urban might have affected how Americans entertained themselves. (*Larger audiences supported larger theaters and stadiums, making mass entertainment possible.*) Tell students to keep this change in mind as they read Part 3.

**Understanding Change Over Time**   Tell students that one of the changes in American life during the 1920s was an increase in leisure time due to changes in working hours and the move to a more urban population. Then have them turn to the Chronology on page 200 and look at entries for the 1920s. Ask them which entries might involve ways Americans of that era used leisure time. Have them suggest categories—entertainment, arts, sports—for these entries, and have students create charts and add information as they read Part 3.

## Geography Connections

Have students use a map of the United States to locate the places named in this chapter about Babe Ruth and other baseball legends. *(Baltimore, Boston, New York, Pittsburgh, Atlanta)* Ask students to discuss why the places named are all cities. *(Only cities could support large stadiums and professional teams.)*

## Meeting Individual Needs

Encourage advanced math students to make a chart of the current career leaders in home runs, batting average, runs batted in, earned run average, or any other significant baseball records.

---

**TEACHING**  *Chapter 9*

# Everyone's Hero
[PAGES 47-50]

**1 Class Period**

### Chapter Summary
Babe Ruth led major league baseball into a new era of popularity, as stars of the national pastime became heroes to millions of Americans.

### Key Vocabulary
leisure time        organized sports        broadcasting

## 1. Connect

Ask students if they have ever heard of Babe Ruth. Who was he? When did he live? (*George Herman Ruth, 1895-1948, known as Babe Ruth, is perhaps the most famous baseball player in history.*) Most students have probably heard of him, even though he died long before they were born.

## 2. Understand

1. Read the main story on pages 47-50. Discuss: How did Babe Ruth help change the game of baseball? (*His hitting power helped change the game from a pitching contest to a hitter's game. His play drew increasing numbers of fans to the game.*)
2. Read the feature on page 50. Discuss: Why was Babe Didrikson Zaharias called the outstanding woman athlete of the first half of the 20th century? (*She was outstanding in baseball, basketball, swimming, tennis, boxing, Olympic track and field, and golf.*)

## 3. Check Understanding

**Writing**   Have students write a tribute to Babe Ruth to place on a wall of a stadium. In the tribute, students should cite his major achievements.

**Thinking About the Chapter (Analyzing)**   Begin a discussion about how changes in American media (radio, movies, newspapers, magazines) helped contribute to the interest in baseball and Babe Ruth. Ask students to think about whether Babe Ruth would have had the same impact if he had lived 50 years earlier.

# Only the Ball
# Was White

[ PAGES 51-54 ]

**1 Class Period**

## Chapter Summary
Kept from the major leagues by Jim Crow attitudes and practices, many black and Hispanic players joined teams in the Negro Leagues, where the quality of play often rivaled or surpassed that in the better-known, all-white leagues.

## Key Vocabulary
barnstorm        Aryan
Jim Crow         misogynist

## 1. Connect

Ask students to name outstanding African American and Hispanic baseball players today. Encourage students to discuss what baseball would be like if major league teams were all-white and African Americans and Hispanic athletes had to play in a different league. Would this be just?

## 2. Understand

1. Read the main text of the chapter. Discuss: Were black and white athletes segregated from the beginning of baseball? (*no*) What led to their segregation? (*After the baseball association fell apart, Cap Anson, a bigot, worked to keep the new leagues for whites only.*) How did men of color respond? (*They formed their own leagues.*)
2. Read the material in boxes and the photo captions. Discuss: Who were some outstanding baseball players of color? (*Josh Gibson, Satchel Paige, Cool Papa Bell, Martin Dihigo, Smokey Joe Williams*) What black athletes were outstanding in other sports? (*Jesse Owens in track and Joe Louis in boxing*)

## 3. Check Understanding

**Writing**  Ask students to write a letter to Cap Anson telling him what they think of segregated baseball.

**Thinking About the Chapter (Hypothesizing)**  Ask students a "what if" question. What if baseball teams were not segregated before 1947? How might that have affected baseball records? How might it have affected attendance at games? How might it have affected which cities had major league baseball teams?

## Reading Nonfiction
*Analyzing Word Choice*

Call students' attention to the literary devices the author uses to describe baseball on page 51. Ask: What analogy describes Satchel Paige's pitching? (*"they say he could have stayed in the strike zone..."*) What analogy shows how fast Cool Papa Bell could run? (*"so fast he could turn off the light switch..."*) What simile describes Gibson's throwing in the photo caption? (*"Throws like a rifle"*) Discuss with students the effect of these literary devices. (*They convey the excitement of the game and the enthusiasm of the player.*)

## More About...
*African Americans in the Baseball Hall of Fame*

Originally, the rules of the Baseball Hall of Fame at Cooperstown, New York, said that a player had to have played on a major league team to be elected to the Hall. That left out some great players who played only in the Negro Leagues. Satchel Paige played in the major leagues after 1948, which made him eligible for the Hall, and he was elected in 1971. The policy was later changed, and the Hall began to recognize players who had never played in the major leagues. In 1972, Josh Gibson was elected by the Committee on Negro Leagues. Other players joined him over time. There is also a Negro League Hall of Fame in Kansas City. Find out more by visiting *www.blackbaseball.com*

## Geography Connections

Distribute Resource Page 3 (TG page 104). Using a map of the United States as a reference, have students mark the following on their outline maps: New Orleans, the Mississippi River, Memphis, St. Louis, Chicago, and other cities where jazz had an early influence.

## Activities/Johns Hopkins Team Learning

See the Student Team Learning Activity on TG page 41.

## Meeting Individual Needs

Encourage musically inclined students to bring instruments or jazz recordings to class and explain to other students some of the musical elements to listen for in a work of jazz.

# American Music

[PAGES 55-62]

**1 Class Period**

## Chapter Summary

The appeal of jazz, a unique musical form developed by African Americans in the South, spread across the nation in the 1920s, thanks to the talents of performers such as Louis Armstrong, Bessie Smith, and King Oliver.

## Key Vocabulary

jazz      Creole      improvisation

## 1. Connect

If possible, play a recording of music by one of the musicians or composers mentioned in this chapter. Then ask students if they can suggest what *jazz* means. They may find jazz difficult to define, but should recognize that it is a kind of music that was born in America.

## 2. Understand

1. Read pages 55-59. Discuss: How does "Jazz Age" describe a period of time? (*It was a period during the 1920s when jazz was the rage. The term was used for the way people lived as well as for the music played.*) Is there any music term that might describe American music today?

2. Read the features on pages 59-61. Discuss: How does the classical music of this time—music composed by Ives and Copland and some of the music by Ellington and Gershwin—differ from jazz? (*Most jazz was improvised; the music in the style of Ives and Copland and the others was written to be played note for note.*) Point out that Ellington and Gershwin also composed some music meant to be played note-for-note; they also composed music that was intended to be improvised. Both Ellington and Gershwin often improvised on their own music.

3. Play a piece of music from this period and ask students to write a paragraph or poem based on the feelings that the music evokes.

## 3. Check Understanding

**Writing**   Ask students to write a paragraph explaining why the author refers to jazz as music that is "uniquely American."

**Thinking About the Chapter (Synthesizing)**   Ask students to make a word web with *Jazz* at the center and various descriptive terms around it.

# Hubba, Hubba, Hubble

[PAGES 63-64]

# Space's Pioneer

[PAGES 65-68]

## 1 Class Period

## Chapter Summary

Edwin Hubble's discoveries set the stage for revolutionary changes in 20th-century science. Robert Goddard provided the first practical proof that space travel might one day be possible.

## Key Vocabulary

Theory of Relativity　　laws of motion　　rocket

## 1. Connect

Ask students what they know about the Hubble Space Telescope (HST), launched into orbit in 1990 to peer into the universe and send back photographs. Explain that the next two chapters tell about pioneers who fixed our attention on outer space.

## 2. Understand

1. Read Chapter 12. Discuss: What were Hubble's most important discoveries about the universe? (*that it is larger than scientists previously imagined; that there are many galaxies; that it is expanding*)
2. Read Chapter 13. Discuss: What did Robert Goddard do on March 16, 1926? (*He launched a rocket.*) Why did he think rockets would be important in the future? (*They would make space travel possible.*) How was Goddard different from other rocket scientists? (*Goddard tested his theories with working models; the others generally worked only with theories.*)

## 3. Check Understanding

**Writing**　　Tell students to write an article about Goddard's first rocket launch, as it might have appeared if a newspaper of the time covered it.

**Thinking About the Chapter (Analyzing)**　　Engage students in a discussion of this question: How can a scientific discovery be considered "revolutionary"? (*if it leads to other discoveries and fundamental changes in ways of thinking*)

## Reading Nonfiction

*Analyzing Text Organization*

Have students go through Chapter 12 to identify the author's pattern of alternating scientific and biographical information.

## More About...

*The Hubble Space Telescope (HST)*

The HST, launched in 1990, was designed to remain in orbit for 15 years. It has been repaired and serviced while in orbit by crews working from the space shuttle. Suggest that students view some of the HST's spectacular images at *www.seds.org/hst/hst.html.* Interested students can investigate the history of the HST by visiting *http://quest.arc.nasa.gov/hst/about.html.*

*Pluto*

Scientists in the late 20th and early 21st centuries started reconsidering whether Pluto is really a planet. It is much smaller than other planets and only slightly larger than some asteroids. Part of the controversy arose from how astronomers define *planet.* Some space centers considered removing its status as a planet. Others decided to wait until a space probe to Pluto was completed.

## Meeting Individual Needs

Ask students who are interested in space science to do research on rockets and report their findings to the class.

## Reading Nonfiction

*Analyzing Rhetorical Devices*

Ask students to discuss how the author makes a persuasive argument that Lindbergh was a hero. Have them identify adjectives that describe Lindbergh on page 73 (*daring, brave, courage, etc.*) and discuss what feelings these words stir up when joined with the word *hero*. For example, what emotions are linked with "a courageous hero?" Point out that the author makes an emotional appeal by using the connotative adjectives. Ask: How does the author also make a logical argument that Lindbergh was a hero? (*She gives facts about Lindbergh that support this and explains why there was a need for an American hero in the 1920s.*)

## Geography Connections

Have students use a globe to trace Lindbergh's flight from New York to Paris. Ask them to identify the latitude and longitude of New York (41°N, 78°W) and Paris (49°N, 2°E). Discuss reasons that knowledge of latitude and longitude is important to pilots, navigators, and explorers.

## Meeting Individual Needs

Ask volunteers to do library research and prepare oral reports on Charles Lindbergh's life after his famous flight.

### NOTE FROM THE AUTHOR

*I believe all teachers need to think across the disciplines and concern themselves with language—even in a history book! You'll find these books give you a rich opportunity to study vocabulary. Ask your students to search for ten words they didn't know, define them, and use each in a sentence. Then have a vocabulary bee.*

---

# The Lone Eagle

[PAGES 69-73]

### 1 Class Period

### Chapter Summary

Charles A. Lindbergh, Jr., became a national—and world—hero when he completed the first nonstop, solo transatlantic flight in 1927 in his single-engine plane the *Spirit of St. Louis*.

### Key Vocabulary

philanthropist          transatlantic

## 1. Connect

Ask students to list qualities that make a person a hero, and list them on the board. (*does a daring deed, captures the imagination, is famous, is a good person, and so on*) Tell them to look for these qualities and others as they read about Charles Lindbergh.

## 2. Understand

1. Read through "He wrote well" on page 71. Discuss: What was Lindbergh about to do? (*be the first to fly from New York to Paris*) What qualifications did he have for this attempt? (*He had flown for years, made parachute jumps, delivered mail, barnstormed showing off trick flying.*)
2. Read the rest of the chapter. Discuss: What preparations did Lindbergh make for the flight? (*He calculated the amount of gasoline he'd need, prepared sandwiches to eat and water to drink, had a rubber raft in case he went down over the ocean, and most important made careful charts of his planned flight.*) Do you think he expected the public attention his flight received? (*He didn't, as evidenced by worrying about whether he could get to Paris from the airport on his own.*)

## 3. Check Understanding

**Writing**   Have students write a list of questions for a reporter to ask Lindbergh about his flight.

**Thinking About the Chapter (Analyzing)**   Engage the class in a discussion of why Lindbergh's flight succeeded and why he became an international hero. (*Students should recognize the importance of good preparation as well as the excitement people felt when he achieved a daring deed that others had attempted and failed.*)

---

## Picturing Words and Music

## 1 Class Period

### Focus Activity

**1.** Read aloud a poem by Langston Hughes or play a jazz recording of Bessie Smith, Louis Armstrong, or Duke Ellington.

**2.** Invite students to comment on the ways in which the poetry or music reflects popular culture in the 1920s.

### Student Team Learning Activity/Representing Information Graphically

**1.** Divide the class into teams. Ask each team to read and research one of the chapters in Part 3 and to decide on the four or five **Big Ideas, Interesting Tidbits, People to Remember,** and **Words to Remember** that best describe its chapter.

**2.** Team members divide up responsibility for the research and each student records information on appropriate note cards. Students also create illustrations for their team's poster. Encourage students to add details and an explanation of why each is important.

**3.** Each team summarizes its chapter information on a handout.

**4.** Each team designs a poster that graphically captures its assigned chapter with illustrations, drawings, or symbols. The poster can be hand-drawn or contain pictures cut from magazines or downloads from web sites.

**5. Circulate and Monitor** Visit each team as the students complete their research, record information on the team's handout, and design their poster. Check that all information is accurate and includes the essential points that other students should know about the chapter.

**6. Sharing Information** Have each team present its handout and poster to the class.

*Making Predictions*

The 1920s seemed to be wonderful times. Americans owned more things than ever before. They also had more leisure time to enjoy them. But trouble lay ahead. By the end of the decade, Will Rogers—a popular comedian who starred on stage, screen, and radio and who wrote for newspapers—could say:

*We've got...more of everything in the world than any nation that ever lived ever had, yet we are starving to death. We are the first nation in the history of the world to go to the poorhouse in an automobile.*

Ask students, basing their ideas on this passage, to guess what happened in America at the end of the 1920s.

# Summarizing Part 3

## Assessing Part 3
**Part 3 Check-Up**   Use Check-Up 3 (TG page 96) to assess student learning in Part 3.

## Alternate Assessment
Ask students to write an outline for a television special about America's heroes during the 1920s.

**Making Connections**   What was the connection between Babe Ruth, Louis Armstrong, Charles Lindbergh, and radio? *(Radio broadcasts spread news about or performances by those people to wider audiences in a shorter time than would have been possible ever before.)*

## Debating the Issues
Use the topic below to stimulate debate.

**Resolved**   That Robert Goddard's accomplishments were greater than those of Charles Lindbergh's, and that he more rightly deserved the fame and praise that Lindbergh received. (Students arguing for Goddard may point out that his ideas and inventions set the groundwork for space exploration, while Lindbergh invented nothing. Students arguing for Lindbergh may point out that his act of personal courage brought the practicality of air travel to wider attention, and that it was not Goddard but later inventors who actually explored space.)

## Making Ethical Judgments
The following activity asks students to consider issues of ethics.

In some New York City nightclubs during the 1920s, blacks could work as entertainers, but were not admitted as customers. If you had been a black entertainer in those years, how would you have responded to a club manager who offered you a job under those terms? (Remind students before they answer that segregation was legal at the time and that work as an entertainer often paid better than other jobs open to African Americans.)

## Projects and Activities
**Designing a Plaque**   Tell students to select one of the sports figures discussed in Chapters 9 and 10, and to design a plaque, complete with illustration and inscription, for that figure.

**Writing a Letter**   Direct students to reread the statement by Lou Gehrig on page 54. Tell them to imagine it is part of a letter that Gehrig is writing to the owner of the New York Yankees urging him to hire black players for the team. The students' assignment is to complete that letter.

**Interpreting a Quote**   Remind students that when asked what jazz is, Louis Armstrong would reply, "If you gotta ask, you'll never know." Have them write brief paragraphs explaining what Armstrong meant by this.

# The Big Ideas

The 1920s had been a time of growth in the nation. But that growth and optimism ended in 1929. Soon people were singing a song that summed up the change:

> They used to tell me I was building a dream
> And so I followed the mob.
> When there was earth to plough or guns to bear
> I was always there right on the job.
> Once I built a railroad, made it run
> Made it race against time,
> Once I built a railroad, now it's done.
> Brother, can you spare a dime?

That song (lyrics by E.Y. Harburg, music by Jay Gorney) became the theme song of the Great Depression. As Americans struggled to cope with economic hardships, they looked to the federal government for assistance. But at first it seemed that the nation's political system was incapable of dealing with such an enormous crisis. Part 4 describes the early years of the Great Depression and its impact on the nation.

# Introducing Part 4

## Setting Goals

Introduce Part 4 by writing its title—"Boom and Bust"—on the chalkboard. Ask students what the boom was. (*the wild prosperity of the 1920s*) Ask them what they think the bust will be. (*the end of that prosperity*)

To set goals for Part 4, tell students that they will
- explain what happened in the stock market and why.
- analyze how the crash started a chain of events.
- describe President Hoover's reaction to the Depression.

## Setting a Context for Reading

**Thinking About the Big Ideas**   Read aloud the lyrics from "Brother, Can You Spare a Dime?" above. Then ask students to summarize what the lyrics express. (*The person speaking had worked hard for the American Dream, helped build America and fought in wars for America, but now there is no work and only strangers to ask for help.*) Tell students that the lyrics are from a song that was one of the most popular of the 1930s and that the lyrics sum up a change that came to the lives of millions of Americans after 1929. In Part 4, students will learn more about that change.

**Identifying Main Idea and Details**   Ask students to read the titles of the four chapters in Part 4. Write each chapter title as a heading of a column on the chalkboard. Tell students the titles are the main ideas—students can rephrase the main ideas, if they choose. As students read the chapter, have them list details that support the main ideas.

# Boom and Bust

## [CHAPTERS 15-18]

## Setting a Context in Space and Time

**Using Maps**  Referring to a wall map of the United States, point out the location of New York City. Challenge students to think of ways that the city is connected to the rest of the nation. (*by roads, railroads, telephone lines, and other forms of communication*) If students have not noted it, point out that there are also economic connections. Tell them that in Part 4 they will learn how one event in New York City in 1929 had a devastating impact on the rest of the nation. Remind students that another event, the attack on the World Trade Center in New York City on September 11, 2001, also had repercussions throughout the country and the world.

**Understanding Change Over Time**  Tell students that these four chapters deal mostly with events in the United States during the years 1928-1932. Have students turn to the Chronology on pages 200-201 and find entries for those years. Ask students to predict, based on those entries, what the chief focus of Chapters 15-18 will be. (*the nation's economy*)

# The Prosperity Balloon

[PAGES 74-75]

**1 Class Period**

## Chapter Summary

Herbert Hoover won the presidential election of 1928 after a campaign in which his supporters pandered to the worst traits of the American voters.

## Key Vocabulary

Ku Klux Klan

## Connect

Calvin Coolidge did not run for reelection in 1928. Herbert Hoover, the Republican candidate, ran against Al Smith, the Democrat.

## Understand

1. Read Chapter 15. Discuss: What qualifications did Herbert Hoover have being president? (*He had been an engineer and businessman, had coordinated relief for starving people in Europe during and after World War I, and had served as U.S. secretary of commerce.*)
2. Discuss: On what grounds did many of Hoover's supporters attack Al Smith during the election campaign? (*Using an anti-city, anti-immigrant approach, they attacked Smith for being Catholic and claimed he wasn't a real American and would take orders from the pope in Rome.*) What other bigots were at large in America at the time? (*Ku Klux Klan: against Catholics, Jews, Asians Arabs, Germans, Irish, Italians, African Americans, and American Indians*)

## Check Understanding

**Writing**   Ask students to write a campaign flyer for Al Smith explaining his qualifications to become president.

**Thinking About the Chapter (Hypothesizing)**   Engage students in a discussion about whether Hoover could have stopped the hate campaign if he chose to. (*There is no easy answer. The issues are whether he controlled the campaign and whether he was willing to risk losing if he stopped the hate.*)

## Geography Connections

Distribute Resource Page 3 (TG page 104). Tell students that the following eight states' electoral votes went to Smith: Alabama, Arkansas, Georgia, Louisiana, Massachusetts, Mississippi, Rhode Island, South Carolina. All the rest went to Hoover. Ask students to use a marker to color the eight states that went to Smith. Discuss their location. What state did Smith come from? (*New York*) Did he win his own state? (*no*)

## Linking Disciplines

*Geography/Math*

Tell students that Hoover received 444 electoral votes, and Smith 87. Ask them to calculate the total electoral vote. (444 + 87 = 531) What percentage of the electoral vote did Smith receive? (16.4%) Use these calculations to discuss the effectiveness of the Hoover campaign.

## Linking Disciplines

*History/Math*

Have students work on these problems. On pages 76-77, how much did Mr. Jones spend on ABC stock? ($1,000) How much money will he have when he sells the stock ($2,000) What will his profit be? ($1,000) On page 75, if Mr. Jones sells 100 shares for $200 each, how much profit will he make? ($10,000)

## Meeting Individual Needs

Have a group of students act out the buying and selling of stocks on margin. Perhaps they can present three scenes: A discussion of margin buying with a stockbroker and the decision to buy on margin. A euphoric scene in which the stock prices rise sharply. The final scene in which the stocks plummet and the stockbroker demands payment of the margin loan.

# Getting Rich Quickly

[PAGES 76-80]

**1 Class Period**

### Chapter Summary

Improving economic conditions in the United States during the 1920s led to a stock market boom. Millions of Americans took part hoping to make quick fortunes. The boom ended in 1929 in a financial panic that marked the beginning of a great economic depression.

### Key Vocabulary

share    bull market      bear market
stock    margin

## 1. Connect

Read the verse at the beginning of Chapter 16. Explain that bulls are people who think the stock market will go up and bears think it will go down. Since the stock market had been rising steadily; many people thought they couldn't lose money by investing.

## 2. Understand

1. Read pages 76-78 through "Then the bulls got frisky." Discuss: What is a share of stock? (*part ownership of a company*) Why do stock prices go up and down? (*Stock prices go up if a company makes money and down if the company loses money.*)
2. Read the rest of the chapter. What does it mean to buy stocks on margin? (*The investor pays part of the price of the stock and borrows the rest.*) How did this cause problems for many people? (*When stock prices fell, people had to pay back the money they had borrowed to buy the stock.*)
3. Discuss: How did the sharp drop in the stock market affect people's property, the banks, and jobs? (*People had to sell property to pay the money they owed for the loans from the brokers; banks lent money to the brokers and lost some of that money; companies closed plants and fired workers.*)

## 3. Check Understanding

**Writing** Ask students to write a diary entry for October 25, 1929, the day after "Black Thursday," for someone who faced losses in the stock market.

**Thinking About the Chapter (Hypothesizing)** Have students discuss whether there was anything that might have kept the economy from crashing in 1929. Ask: would investors who were making fortunes in the stock market have listened to any warnings? (*Students will probably agree that it's human nature to ignore warnings when things are going well.*)

# Down and Out

[PAGES 81-85]

**1 Class Period**

## Chapter Summary

During the Great Depression, huge numbers of Americans suffered and struggled to find ways to cope as they lost jobs, savings, and homes. Among the hardest hit were the farmers of the Great Plains, as crop prices fell and droughts and dust storms ravaged once-valuable farmland.

## Key Vocabulary

depression    Dust Bowl
Hoovervilles    crop rotation

## 1. Connect

The Great Depression affected people in cities and on farms. Many people were out of work or working part time. Many lost their homes. Read the Studs Terkel quotation at the beginning of the chapter. Discuss with students his comment, "The Depression is an embarrassing thing." Ask students why they think it was "embarrassing."

## 2. Understand

1. Read pages 81-83. Discuss: How did the Depression affect people in cities? (*Many lost their jobs and then their homes. Food was scarce.*) What happened on farms during this period? (*Prices of farm products dropped, and many farmers destroyed crops rather than sell produce at less than it cost to grow.*)
2. Read the rest of the chapter. Discuss: What created the Dust Bowl? (*Poor soil management led to soil being blown away by dust storms, leaving poor land for farming.*) Where did many people who lost their homes live? (*They built shacks of boxes and boards in places they called Hoovervilles.*)

## 3. Check Understanding

**Writing**   Ask students to write a news article describing a Hooverville and the people who live there and including an explanation of why Hoovervilles exist.

**Thinking About the Chapter (Evaluating)**   Ask students for their opinions on whether urban or rural areas suffered the most after the crash. (*While farmers might be able to raise food for their families, the loss of soil could have made farming impossible. Urban families that depended on factory jobs had no ready source of food. In both cases, people may have had to leave their homes.*)

## Reading Nonfiction

*Analyzing Graphic Devices*

Ask students to write a sentence about each painting or photograph in the chapter. Have them tell which element of the work most strongly conveys to them the gravity of the Great Depression. (*the skin-and-bones cow in the painting on page 84; the people's expressions in the Lange photograph on page 83*)

## Geography Connections

Distribute Resource Page 3 (TG page 104). Then use a map of the United States to help students identify the Great Plains area that was part of the Dust Bowl. Have students shade areas on their maps to show the extent of the Dust Bowl—stretching over southeastern Colorado, southwestern Kansas, the Texas and Oklahoma panhandles, and northeastern New Mexico. Explain that the federal government supported programs to plant windbreaks and encourage good soil management. These helped the area recover.

## Activities/Johns Hopkins Team Learning

See the Student Team Learning Activity on TG page 49.

## History Archives

*A History of US Sourcebook*
#75, Herbert Hoover, *"Rugged Individualism": Campaign Speech in New York City* (1928)

## Linking Disciplines

*History/Music*

Play aloud some songs of the Depression era by Woody Guthrie. Then challenge students to create their own lyrics describing some aspect of the Great Depression.

## Reading Nonfiction

*Analyzing Primary and Secondary Sources*

Ask a volunteer to read the Hoover quotations on page 86, and then invite the class to speculate on whether Hoover solved the "Economic Disaster" (the Great Depression) referred to in the chapter's title. After reading the chapter, again refer students to the quotations. Ask: Why did the author place these quotes at the beginning of the chapter? (*The quotes show how wrong-headed Hoover's ideas were; the quotes stand in stark contrast to all the information about the Depression the author gives in the text.*)

## Meeting Individual Needs

Ask independent learners to research and prepare oral reports on the effects of the Great Depression on a specific group, such as African Americans, Hispanics, Native Americans, or various immigrant groups.

# Economic Disaster

[PAGES 86-89]

**1 Class Period**

## Chapter Summary

The crisis of the Great Depression threatened both the political and the economic systems under which the United States operated, especially when it became apparent that President Hoover had no bold new ideas for meeting the challenge the nation faced.

## Key Vocabulary

Bonus Army      pacifist      voluntarism

### 1. Connect

Ask the students when—if ever—the government should help its citizens recover from a disaster. Ask students if anyone they know has received assistance after a flood or other disaster. Explain that the question of whether government should help people during the Great Depression was the question President Hoover faced.

### 2. Understand

1. Read pages 86-87. Discuss: What did President Hoover say about the economy from 1930 to 1932? (*He said that it was recovering and the government should not help individuals.*) Ask: Why did thousands of veterans march on Washington, D.C.? (*Many didn't have jobs and wanted the government to pay them their promised bonuses then instead of in 1945.*)
2. Read the rest of the chapter. Discuss: Do you think President Hoover was in a position to understand what was happening to millions of people? (*Students might suggest that since he was living well, he didn't really understand the suffering of millions of individuals.*) Discuss: Why did some people of the 1930s report favorably on dictators in Europe? (*Some people thought the U.S. economic and political systems had failed and only a strong leader could solve the nation's problems.*)

### 3. Check Understanding

**Writing**   Ask students to write a letter to President Hoover that a veteran might have written to explain the problem and ask for or suggest solutions.

**Thinking About the Chapter (Analyzing)**   Why do you think the army attacked the Bonus Army? (*Although President Hoover said he saved the country from mob action, he was probably afraid of a revolution even though the Bonus Army was acting peacefully.*) Should President Hoover have spoken to representatives of the Bonus Army? (*Answers will vary.*)

## Surviving the Great Depression

## 1 Class Period

### Focus Activity

**1.** Ask students to use **Think-Pair-Share** to discuss answers to this question:

*What would you do if suddenly your family had no income and there were no unemployment insurance, social security, or bank account to fall back on?*

Make sure students realize that in the early 1930s those protections did not exist. Divide the class into teams and direct students to examine the illustrations and read the captions in Chapter 17 to discover what some people did to survive the Great Depression.

**2.** Use **Numbered Heads** for the teams to briefly report their findings to the class.

### Student Team Learning Activity/Making Comparisons

**1.** Distribute Resource Page 5 (TG page 106) to teams. Review the information provided on the Resource Page. Make sure students look at the prices in the *Price Then* column in the context of the *Weekly Wages (Then)*. Assign teams one or two categories of Household Articles and ask them to research and complete the *Price Now* column for those categories.

**2.** Assign each team one of the occupations listed under *Then and Now: Wages*. Ask the team to design a monthly budget which would allow the worker's family to buy (or save up for) adult winter coats, a gas stove, and toys for their four children. Direct teams to assume that half of the weekly salary for each occupation would be used for rent and food. (The portion of a salary that went for rent and food actually varied widely). Have teams share their budgets and savings plans with the class. As a follow-up, ask students what would happen to each family's budget if its weekly wages were suddenly cut in half.

**3.** If possible, obtain a copy of *Hard Times* by Studs Terkel. Assign each student a first-person account of life during the Great Depression to read aloud.

**4.** Ask each student to write a one- or two-sentence summary impression of their first-person account or to choose one or two powerful sentences from it. (For instance, "The auctioneers came and took our last cow, which I had named. I stood crying in the window.") Have each student write these sentences on sentence strips to be combined in a class poem, "Voices of the Great Depression."

## Looking Ahead

*Interpreting a Quote*

Many years after the Great Depression, an African American man was asked how blacks felt about politics in those troubled years. He replied:

> *My father told me: "The Republicans are the ship. All else is the sea." Frederick Douglass said that. The [blacks] didn't go for Roosevelt much in '32. But the WPA came along and Roosevelt came to be a god.*

Ask students what they think the statement by Frederick Douglass means. (*The Republican party, which was the party of Lincoln, offered the only safety and security for blacks.*) How did black political support shift after 1932? (*Blacks came to support Roosevelt and, by extension, the Democratic party.*) Tell students that in Part 5 they will learn more about how Roosevelt won the support of black voters and about how many other Americans came to share the feelings expressed in the quote.

# Summarizing Part 4

## Assessing Part 4

**Part 4 Check-Up**  Use Check-Up 4 (TG page 97) to assess student learning in Part 4.

## Alternate Assessment

Ask students to create a flow chart showing the chain of events that led to the Great Depression and the collapse of the U.S. economy.

**Making Connections**  Imagine that President Hoover has appointed you to a special commission investigating the effects of the stock market crash on the nation. One of the commission's goals is to determine whether urban or rural areas have suffered most in the changes that followed the crash. How would your report read? (*Students might keep in mind that farmers, if they kept their farms, could often at least grow food for themselves and their families, while people in cities could not.*)

## Debating the Issues

Use the topic below to stimulate debate.

**Resolved**  That Herbert Hoover acted correctly in breaking up the Bonus Army. (To stimulate discussion, assign students these roles: Hoover and his aides, MacArthur and other army officers, Washington police, members of the Bonus Army.)

## Making Ethical Judgments

The following activity asks students to consider issues of ethics.

President Hoover said that no government money should be spent on relief programs. Do you think he was right at first? Should he have re-thought his position as hunger grew worse? (Opinions will vary. Ask students to think of a farmer who lost the farm, a factory worker who lost a job, a veteran who had been promised a bonus, a business owner who is barely surviving.)

## Projects and Activities

**Designing Campaign Posters**  Divide students into four groups. Assign groups to design campaign posters that might have been used in the 1928 presidential campaigns of Hoover and Smith and the 1932 campaigns of Hoover and Roosevelt.

**Writing Letters**  Divide the class into two groups. Ask students in one group to imagine that they live in the Dust Bowl in the early 1930s. Ask the group to imagine that they are relatives of those in the first group who live in a Northeastern industrial city that has been heavily hit by plant closings. Have the two groups write and exchange letters describing what life is like for them during the Depression.

**Creating a Mural**  Tell students to review the chapters in Part 4 and then draw a mural of scenes illustrating events of the Depression from the 1929 crash to the 1932 election.

## The Big Ideas

# PART 5

# Rendezvous with Destiny

## [CHAPTERS 19–25]

On the night of June 27, 1936, more than 100,000 people packed the stadium at Philadelphia's Franklin Field. That night, Franklin Delano Roosevelt accepted the Democratic nomination to run for a second term as president. In a clear, calm voice, Roosevelt declared:

> *There is a mysterious cycle in human events. To some generations much is given. Of other generations much is expected. This generation of Americans has a rendezvous with destiny....*

Amid a time of despair, Roosevelt filled Americans with hope. His promise to promote economic and political justice won him an unprecedented four terms as president. Part 5 traces Roosevelt's personal "rendezvous with destiny" and the changes that he brought to the United States political system.

## Introducing Part 5

### Setting Goals

Introduce Part 5 by reading the Roosevelt quotation above to the class. Write "Rendezvous with Destiny" on the chalkboard and define *rendezvous* (an appointment) and *destiny* (fate). Ask students what they think Roosevelt meant by this phrase. Write some possible interpretations on the chalkboard, then suggest students think again about the meaning of the phrase after they read Chapters 19-25.

To set goals for Part 5, tell students that they will

- examine the backgrounds and characters of Franklin Delano Roosevelt and Eleanor Roosevelt.
- analyze the effects of FDR's crippling polio and his efforts to overcome them.
- compare and contrast FDR's and Hoover's attitudes toward government intervention in the U.S. economy.

### Setting a Context for Reading

**Thinking About the Big Ideas**   You might begin Part 5 by referring students to the painting on page 105 and the caption below it. Call on a student to read the caption aloud. Ask: What does the Will Rogers quote tell you about people's attitude toward change in 1933? (*They favored change.*) Explore how Rogers used humor to get this point across. (*By saying that Americans might even cheer Roosevelt if he set fire to the Capitol, Rogers indicated that Americans wanted someone to do something.*) Ask students to recall information from Part 4 (Chapters 15-18). What social and economic injustices might have fueled this desire for change? (*discrimination against blacks and immigrants, wide gaps between the rich and poor, skyrocketing unemployment, and so on*)

**Comparing and Contrasting**   As students read Chapters 19-25, encourage them to make a list comparing and contrasting Hoover and Roosevelt with regard to personality, philosophy of government, relationship with the American people, previous government experience, and other aspects students introduce.

## Setting a Context in Space and Time

**Using Maps**   To link Parts 4 and 5, distribute Resource Page 3 (TG page 104). Have students use a marker to shade in the states won by Hoover in the 1932 election (Maine, New Hampshire, Vermont, Connecticut, Pennsylvania, and Delaware). Have students write *Roosevelt Country* across the rest of the map. Ask students to suggest reasons, based on the closing chapters of Part 4, why so much of the nation lined up behind Roosevelt in 1932. Tell students to imagine that they lived in Roosevelt Country. What might they expect from the new president? What characteristics do students think would best help Roosevelt to fulfill these expectations? Compare students' responses with the personality traits listed on page 105.

**Understanding Change Over Time**   Set a time frame for Part 5 by writing *generation* on the chalkboard. Explore what this word means to students. (*all the people born and living at about the same time*) Tell students that the average period between generations is considered to be about 30 years. Ask students in what decade their generation was born. In what decade will they reach voting age—age 18?

Next, point out that the generation that came of voting age—21 at that time—in the 1930s was born in the 1910s. Have students use the Chronology on pages 200-201 to suggest some of the big events that may have influenced the thinking of that generation. Then read aloud the quotation by Roosevelt on TG page 51. Ask students whether young adults in the 1930s belonged to a generation to which "much is given" or a generation from which "much is expected." What events in the Chronology support students' answers?

# A Boy Who Loved History

[PAGES 90-91]

# How About This?

[PAGES 92-94]

**1 Class Period**

## Chapter Summaries

From an early age, family stories connected Franklin Delano Roosevelt with the nation's past. Although Roosevelt came from a privileged background, his family instilled in him honesty, kindness, and religious faith. These values gave him the courage to tackle frustrations ranging from a crippling bout of polio to the challenges of national politics.

## Key Vocabulary

poliomyelitis     infantile paralysis

## 1. Connect

Have students preview the photos and captions in Chapters 19 and 20. Discuss the affluent lifestyle represented in the photos. Ask students if they would expect a child of such privilege to understand and sympathize with the situation of people suffering during the Great Depression.

## 2. Understand

1. Read Chapter 19. Discuss: How did young Franklin learn about the history of his country? (*through family stories*) What did he admire about Thomas Jefferson and Alexander Hamilton? (*Jefferson's concern for the average citizen and Hamilton's belief in a strong federal government*)
2. Read Chapter 20. Discuss: Who were some people who influenced young Franklin? (*his parents and his uncle Theodore Roosevelt*) What character trait showed courage? (*He never complained when he was hurt or troubled.*)

## 3. Check Understanding

**Writing**   Have students write a paragraph telling why Franklin might have chosen a life that was different from the life his parents expected him to live.

**Thinking About the Chapter (Synthesizing)**   Ask students to discuss the various influences on young Franklin Roosevelt and to suggest the way each might have affected the way he grew up.

## Reading Nonfiction

*Analyzing Point of View*

Read aloud Roosevelt's statements in the side-notes on pages 90 and 91. Ask: How might Roosevelt's point of view on immigrants affect his presidency? (*He would be inclusive and non-discriminatory.*) Encourage students to discuss how his attitude toward immigrants and religious beliefs reflect the Constitution. Then have students compare his views with those of the people who ran Hoover's election campaign (*page 74*). Discuss how the public's attitude might have changed during Hoover's presidency. (*The Depression may have lessened such mean-spiritedness.*)

## Linking Disciplines

*History/Science*

Have students use the library and/or Internet to learn more about polio, how it affected people, and why it is now rare in the United States and the developed world. Some students may be interested in researching areas of Africa and Asia where polio is still active and severe. Many of these areas are torn by war.

## A Lonely Little Girl
[PAGES 95-96]

## First Lady
## of the World
[PAGES 97-98]

**1 Class Period**

### Chapter Summaries
Elliot Roosevelt inspired his daughter Eleanor with his dreams of the woman she would one day become. Eleanor never lost sight of these dreams as she struggled to overcome the fears and insecurities of a painful childhood. Franklin and Eleanor Roosevelt formed one of the great political teams in history. When polio crippled FDR, Eleanor became his legs, eyes, and ears.

### Key Vocabulary
Second Bonus Army                    underdog
Civilian Conservation Corps (CCC)

### 1. Connect

Franklin Roosevelt grew up in a wealthy family with many material advantages. So did his distant cousin Eleanor Roosevelt. But while Franklin was surrounded by a loving family, Eleanor faced loss of loved ones and coldness. Nevertheless two people—her father and a school principal—encouraged her to be the best person she could be.

### 2. Understand

1. Read Chapter 21. Discuss: What difficulties did Eleanor face during her childhood? (*lack of attention from mother, father's alcoholism, deaths of parents and a brother, grandmother who didn't understand children, mean governess*) What influences helped Eleanor overcome these problems? (*her father's dreams for her future, Marie Souvestre's encouragement*)

2. Read Chapter 22. Discuss: How did Eleanor Roosevelt change the role of the First Lady? (*She acted as FDR's legs, eyes, and ears, kept him informed about government projects and public opinion; she wrote a newspaper column and books; she held regular press conferences and campaigned for minority rights.*)

### 3. Check Understanding

**Writing**   Ask students to write a job description for the First Lady, using Eleanor Roosevelt as a model.

**Thinking About the Chapter (Analyzing)**   Ask students to analyze the influences and experiences that might have led Eleanor Roosevelt to create a new role for the First Lady.

# Handicap or Character Builder?

[PAGES 99-101]

# Candidate Roosevelt

[PAGES 102-103]

**1 Class Period**

## Chapter Summary

Although polio crippled Roosevelt, it gave him a strength and courage that would mold his presidency. At the 1932 Democratic National Convention, Roosevelt pledged a "new deal for the American people."

## Key Vocabulary

character          dilettante          New Deal

## 1. Connect

Ask students how people react to a handicap or disability. Discuss reasons why people react differently to handicaps.

## 2. Understand

1. Read Chapter 23. Discuss: How did FDR respond to a crippling attack of polio? (*He tried to build himself up as much as possible; he found ways to regain some physical independence; he refused to act like an invalid.*) In what ways did his disability make FDR a better candidate? (*He was forced to become focused and serious, "steady in his views."*)
2. Read Chapter 24. Discuss: What problems threatened the United States when FDR took office? (*Problems included bank closings, hoarding of gold, growing fear that the government would not be able to meet its payroll.*) What were some of the Progressive ideas on which the New Deal was built? (*opposition to monopoly; belief that the government should help regulate the economy; the idea that most poverty arises from social problems*)

## 3. Check Understanding

**Writing**   Ask students to write a paragraph describing how FDR tried to keep his life as normal as possible after he survived polio.

**Thinking About the Chapter (Identifying the Main Idea)**   Discuss why it was so important for FDR to break with tradition and appear personally at the Democratic National Convention to accept the party's nomination. (*to show he was physically mobile, to shake off the "horse-and-buggy" ways of doing things and immediately declare a "new deal" for new times*)

## Reading Nonfiction

*Analyzing Word Choice*

Have students read the feature on page 100. Ask them to analyze why Roosevelt's choice of wording was better than the official's. (*It was more direct and clear.*) Ask students to find an overly complicated instruction or notice and to rewrite it in direct language.

## More About...

*FDR's Disability*

Although FDR never tried to pretend he was not crippled, he did not like to be photographed in his wheelchair or with his braces showing, and he didn't want to be photographed walking with difficulty. His preference led to a controversy when the Roosevelt Memorial was built in Washington, D.C. Many groups of handicapped people wanted to show Roosevelt in a wheelchair because they thought it would inspire people to overcome disabilities. Many historians, however, believed that showing the wheelchair would be against the wishes of the president. FDR was finally shown seated with a cape that covers his legs and wheelchair. Students can see the memorial on the Internet at *www.nps.gov/fdrm.*

## Linking Disciplines

*Geography/Technology*

Point out that FDR was making his airplane trip from Albany to Chicago in 1932, only 5 years after Lindbergh's transatlantic flight. Plane travel was not yet common. As the note on page 72 explains, it would not be until 1939 that the first commerical passenger flight would take off from New York to Marseilles.

## Meeting Individual Needs

Ask students who are visual learners to examine the cartoons on page 103 and explain why they are effective. Encourage students to discuss both the words and the particular details of the artwork.

## Reading Nonfiction

*Analyzing Rhetorical Devices*

Discuss with students that one way writers or speakers try to capture the audience's attention or to explain a new idea is to make an analogy that is fresh and interesting. What comparisons does the author make in her analogy on pages 104-105? (*compares the American economy to the patient; Dr. Leave Alone to people who were against the New Deal; and Dr. New Deal to Roosevelt*) Have partners write a sentence explaining why comparing the economy to a sick patient is an effective way to personalize the need for economic relief at that time.

## Activities/Johns Hopkins Team Learning

See the Student Team Learning Activity on TG page 57.

## History Archives

*A History of US Sourcebook*

#76, From Franklin D. Roosevelt, *"The Only Thing We Have to Fear Is Fear Itself": First Inaugural Address* (1933)

## Meeting Individual Needs

Ask independent learners to read the feature on page 107 and identify the programs that still exist today. Suggest that they select one existing New Deal program to investigate. Ask them to make a chart showing the main points of the program and how people today benefit from it.

Have students who need practice speaking prepare a fireside chat in which Franklin or Eleanor Roosevelt addresses the nation over radio. Franklin's chat should recap actions during his first 100 days in office. Eleanor's chat should discuss the need for justice for all Americans.

# President Roosevelt

[PAGES 104-108]

**1 Class Period**

## Chapter Summary

FDR swept into office with a whirlwind agenda for change. His New Deal programs actively involved government in the lives of citizens and shared power with people who had never held it before. FDR's reshaping of the U.S. political system set off a debate over big government that continues to this day.

## Key Vocabulary

brain trust       Social Security

## 1. Connect

Read the feature on page 104 aloud. Ask students to explain why these words would have given hope to Americans.

## 2. Understand

1. Read through the first two lines on page 106. Discuss: How did Roosevelt's ideas on the Depression differ from those of Coolidge and Hoover? (*Coolidge and Hoover believed that nothing could or should be done and the economy would correct itself. Roosevelt believed that the government had to try new ideas.*)
2. Read the rest of the chapter. Discuss: How did the New Deal change some of America's business habits? (*Possible answers: The New Deal ended child labor, regulated the stock market, guaranteed bank deposits, regulated wages, encouraged unions, limited work hours, helped farmers, increased social welfare.*) How did FDR increase citizens' involvement in the political system? (*He brought into power people who had not held power before—women, blacks, Eastern Europeans, southern Europeans, American Indians, Catholics, and Jews.*)

## 3. Check Understanding

**Writing**   Ask students to write a short news article about the appointment of Frances Perkins as the first woman cabinet officer.

**Thinking About the Chapter (Recognizing Different Perspectives)**   Point out that some Americans supported FDR and the New Deal, while others were highly critical. Engage students in a discussion about which groups would be most likely to hold one opinion or another. (*People who were suffering most from the Depression would be likely supporters, while those who were not suffering would have been most likely to oppose the policies. Also, people who had formerly been locked out of power would have been supporters, while the old power elite might have been opposed.*)

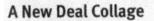

## A New Deal Collage

### 1 Class Period

#### Focus Activity

Discuss with students the ways government impacts their lives. To start the discussion, mention areas of governmental influence, such as national security, taxation, consumer protection, transportation, and communications. Then ask students to specify the ways the federal government is involved in these areas.

#### Student Team Learning Activity/Creating a Collage

**1.** Divide the class into teams. Distribute Resource Page 6 (TG page 107). Inform students that each team will decide which are the ten most valuable or important New Deal programs, using information on the Resource Page and in the feature on page 107.

**2.** Once the teams decide on their "top ten," have each team create a collage poster illustrating their choices and title it. (For example, "The New Deal Big Ten" or "The Most Important Alphabet Soup Programs.") The collage should include one or more pictures or illustrations related to the goals or achievements of each of the ten New Deal programs or agencies. Students may cut pictures from magazines and newspapers or draw illustrations representing the programs. (For example, young men building a road might illustrate the CCC; photographs of senior citizens might illustrate the Social Security Act.)

**3.** Have each team assemble the illustrations on poster paper and neatly write captions that include the name of the agency or program and a one-sentence description of the goal or achievement symbolized by the illustration.

**4. Circulate and Monitor** While the teams are working, systematically visit each one to assist students with reading and finding appropriate pictures for the programs.

**5. Sharing Information** Have teams present their posters to the class, explaining the significance of their choices. Then create a class display of the posters.

## Looking Ahead

*Making Predictions*

Have students summarize the most important domestic crisis facing the United States in the late 1930s. Then read the following selection from the November 10, 1938, edition of the *Chicago Tribune*:

> *Systematic destruction of Jewish property, looting, arson, and wholesale arrests of Jews without official charges swept Germany today. It is estimated that 20,000 Jews were arrested....*

What does this story tell students about events in Europe around that time? What violations of justice does the story reveal? How do students think the United States might respond? Save student predictions to compare with information in Part 6.

# Summarizing Part 5

## Assessing Part 5

**Part 5 Check-Up**    Use Check-Up 5 (TG page 98) to assess student learning in Part 5.

## Alternate Assessment

Ask students to write an essay about how Roosevelt broke with the past.

**Making Connections**    What influences or experiences in Franklin Roosevelt's early life might have encouraged him to bring bold changes to government? *(confidence and optimism inspired by FDR's family, tendency to see problems as challenges to be solved, patience and courage from his battle with polio, etc.)*

## Debating the Issues

Use the topic below to stimulate debate.

**Resolved**    That it is not appropriate to try programs that may or may not work when the nation is facing a crisis. (Appoint students to represent the view that the nation should not be used as a testing laboratory. Appoint other students to represent the view that doing something is better than doing nothing, and that some programs may work.)

## Making Ethical Judgments

The following activity asks students to consider issues of ethics.

On page 92, the author asks students to put themselves in Franklin Roosevelt's shoes as a child. If they had enjoyed his wealth, would they have turned out differently than he did? (Joy Hakim points out the effect of good values upon FDR's character. Following this line of thought, you might have students identify some of the values that promote civic responsibility. Ask students how a democratic nation such as the United States might teach young people these values.)

## Projects and Activities

**Writing Biographical Entries**    Tell students to write biographical entries on Franklin and Eleanor Roosevelt. Each entry can be no more than 125 words long. Students should begin by listing key facts about each person's life. Have students put the most important facts at the beginning, so that they can eliminate items toward the end if the entries run long.

**Completing a News Story**    Distribute this incomplete news story from the November 14, 1932, edition of *Time* magazine:

> *Throughout the length & breadth of the land, some 40,000,000 citizens were proceeding in quiet, orderly fashion to cast their ballots in the memorable Depression election of 1932....*

Assign students to use information from Part 5 to complete this election-day story from the past.

## The Big Ideas

In the late 1930s, the global peacekeeping system began to break down. President Roosevelt privately talked about shifting roles from Dr. New Deal to Dr. Win the War. In October 1937, he told Americans about a disease more deadly than the Depression. Roosevelt warned:

> It seems to be unfortunately true that the epidemic of world lawlessness is spreading....War is a contagion, whether it be declared or undeclared. It can engulf states and peoples remote from the original scene of hostilities. We are determined to keep out of war, yet we cannot...have complete protection in a world of disorder....

FDR hoped to awaken Americans to the dangers of foreign aggression. But most Americans considered distant dictators less threatening than the economic crisis at home. Part 6 explores events that led the United States out of isolation and into a conflict in which competing political systems vied for world power.

# PART 6
# The World in Flames
## [CHAPTERS 26-32]

## Introducing Part 6

### Setting Goals

Introduce Part 6 by writing the title, "The World in Flames," on the chalkboard. Ask students if they can figure out to what this title refers. (*the beginning of World War II*) Ask students to flash back in time to the end of World War I and Woodrow Wilson's hopes for "a just peace" and saving the world for democracy. Ask students to suggest some aspects of the aftermath of World War I that might have laid a groundwork for World War II. (*harsh reparations for Germany, failure of the United States to join the League of Nations, lack of self-determination for small nations, etc.*)

To set goals for Part 6, tell students that they will
- describe the rise of European dictators and analyze reasons for their emergence at that time.
- debate whether other European countries or the United States should have intervened in the early aggression of the dictatorships.
- discuss the Nazi war against Jews.
- explain the circumstances that led the isolationist United States to participate in World War II.

### Setting a Context for Reading

**Thinking About the Big Ideas**   You might open Part 6 by reading aloud the quote from Roosevelt above. Ask students what analogy, or comparison, Roosevelt uses to describe war. (*epidemic or highly contagious disease*) What does Roosevelt imply are the symptoms of this disease? (*lawlessness, disorder*) Now reread the report from the *Chicago Tribune* in Summarizing Part 5 (TG page 58). Do students think this report confirms

Roosevelt's diagnosis of global ills? Why or why not? Ask students what type of political system might approve such attacks against a people. (*dictatorship*) Use students' speculations to lead into Chapter 26.

**Using Primary and Secondary Sources**   Remind students that Joy Hakim has based her book on many primary and secondary sources. She has also included a wealth of primary sources—words and images written and made at or shortly after an event by people who were there. Ask students to look through Chapters 26-32 to identify primary visual sources. As students read Part 6, they should identify the primary sources and discuss what can be learned from them.

## Setting a Context in Space and Time

**Using Maps**   Distribute Resource Page 4 (TG page 105) and refer students to the map on page 135. Ask them to identify the continents and bodies of water upon which World War II was fought, and to use the map in their books to fill in their outline maps. Do students think it would have been possible for the United States to stay out of this conflict? Why or why not? Tell students that Chapters 26-32 trace events that shattered U.S. illusions about the nation's ability to remain isolated from conflicts abroad.

**Using a Time Line**   Remind students of the differences between underlying and immediate causes. (Underlying causes usually build up over time; immediate causes are events that trigger a change.) Next, tell students that World War II began in 1939 when Germany invaded Poland. But the seeds for war were planted much earlier. Have students review their time line for Book Nine. What is the earliest underlying cause of World War II that they can identify? (Encourage students to link the Versailles Treaty and the U.S. refusal to join the League of Nations with the outbreak of World War II.) Have students identify other items on the time line that may have contributed to a second global war. Mark these items with an arrow pointed toward 1939. As students add items from Part 6 to the time line, have them continue to mark underlying causes with an arrow.

If students have not already constructed a time line for Book Nine, have them begin one for the periods covered by Parts 6-8 (1932-1946). In addition to having students identify the causes of World War II, have them place small U.S. flags on events directly involving the United States. Use these flags to help students draw conclusions about the effect of U.S. involvement on the outcome of the war.

# Twentieth-Century Monsters

[PAGES 109-113]

## 1 Class Period

## Chapter Summary
As an antidote to economic depression, some nations turned to militant nationalism. War machines fueled by hatred became the tools of dictators.

## Key Vocabulary

| | | |
|---|---|---|
| Nazism | Fascism | Communism |
| reparations | nationalism | totalitarian |

## 1. Connect

The United States now sends troops to keep the peace in other countries when we are not at war. Some Americans object to this. Others believe that it is necessary to prevent a larger war. Ask students to hypothesize about the consequences of sending troops and of not sending troops.

## 2. Understand

1. Read pages 109-111 up to "and most believed him." Discuss: What changes did Hitler bring to Germany's political system? (*He had the Reichstag give him absolute power as a dictator.*) Why did many Germans support Hitler's rise to power? (*Most Germans believed their leaders, who said Germany had been unfairly blamed for World War I and they felt humiliated by the Versailles Treaty. They also wanted a strong leader to end Germany's economic chaos.*)

2. Read the rest of the chapter. Discuss: In which other countries did militant nationalism and totalitarian government take hold? (*Japan, Spain, Italy, Soviet Union*) Discuss: How does a totalitarian system differ from a democratic system? (*In a totalitarian state, people don't matter; only the state is important. In a democracy, the government is based on the consent of the people.*)

## 3. Check Understanding

**Writing**   Ask students to write a paragraph explaining what a totalitarian state is, using examples from the chapter.

**Thinking About the Chapter (Understanding Cause and Effect)**
Point out that the Great Depression affected many countries. Ask students why they think the response to the depression led to a dictatorship in some countries and strengthened democracies in other countries.

## Reading Nonfiction

*Analyzing Text Organization*

Have students re-read the last paragraph in the chapter. Then ask: What were the causes of totalitarianism in Germany, Italy, Japan, and the U.S.S.R.? Point out that the author has loosely organized this chapter by cause-and-effect. Then ask partners to list some of the causes that led to the rise of totalitarianism in each of the above-mentioned countries.

## Geography Connections

Distribute Resource Page 4 (TG page 105). Ask students to examine the map on page 112, and to transfer information to their outline maps using different color pencils for different dates. Have students locate Germany and the neighbors affected by its aggression and mark them on their maps. Point out that this map shows only German aggression in Europe. It does not show Italy's aggression in North Africa or Japan's aggression in China.

## Geography Connections

Distribute Resource Page 4 (TG page 105). Have students make a list of places mentioned in the text and then locate the places and the present-day countries where they are located. Have them show this information on their outline maps.

## Meeting Individual Needs

Encourage advanced students to read the feature on page 115 and use the information there and in the First Amendment to come up with a statement on religious freedom in the United States. Some students may be interested in going beyond these sources to learn more about legal cases involving religious freedom.

## Activities/Johns Hopkins Team Learning

See the Student Team Learning Activity on TG page 68.

# A Final Solution

[ PAGES 112-119 ]

**1 Class Period**

### Chapter Summary

Anti-Semitism had existed for centuries. But in Nazi Germany it took on new dimensions of evil. As Hitler undertook a methodical and ruthless destruction of the Jews, racism and bigotry within other nations kept the world largely silent.

### Key Vocabulary

| | | |
|---|---|---|
| anti-Semitism | eugenics | Aryan |
| Kristallnacht | xenophobia | Inquisition |

## 1. Connect

Have a volunteer read aloud to the class the quotation from Henry A. Overstreet on page 114. Ask students to discuss the idea that permitting evil is committing evil.

## 2. Understand

1. Read pages 114-117 through "Hitler was soon giving it away." Discuss: What does the author cite as some of the possible origins of anti-Semitism? (*intolerance of Jews' non-comforming political attitudes, their refusal to convert to other religions, jealousy of the economic success of some Jews, rise of the pseudo-science of racism*)
2. Read the rest of the chapter. Discuss: How did the Nazis carry anti-Semitism to new levels of wickedness? (*They used modern technology in an attempt to eradicate an entire people.*) Why did the United States block the entry of large numbers of Jewish refugees? (*Answers will vary. Help students understand that even democratic nations are not free of xenophobia and prejudice.*)

## 3. Check Understanding

**Writing**   Ask students to write a letter to the editor of a newspaper in 1939 explaining why the United States should accept 20,000 children fleeing from Nazi persecution.

**Thinking About the Chapter (Sequencing)**   Ask students to make a chart showing the intensification of persecution of Jews by the Nazis from 1933 though the 1940s. (*1933: boycott of Jewish businesses; Hitler blamed Jews for economic problems; took Jewish property; 1938: Kristallnacht; 1939: Jews had to wear yellow Star of David; 1940: concentration camp; 1942: Jews across Europe rounded up and transported to gas chambers in Poland at Auschwitz and Maidanek.*) Then discuss the question posed on page 119: "Did all this have anything to do with the United States?"

# War
# and the Scientists

[PAGES 122-123]

*NOTE FROM THE AUTHOR*

*Set up a TV talk show. The moderator is a news reporter; the guests are experts on an event of the time. Have your "experts" prepare statements and then expect to answer "call-in questions" from the classroom audience.*

## 1 Class Period

### Chapter Summary

A group of scientists discovered a way to unleash the power of the atom. The decision to use this power as a weapon of war was one of the most awesome—and agonizing—decisions of modern times.

### Key Vocabulary

theory of relativity

## 1. Connect

Among the refugees who fled totalitarian Europe were scientists, many of them Jews. The most notable was Albert Einstein. He and most of the others became U.S. citizens and many helped the effort to win the war.

## 2. Understand

1. Read the chapter. Discuss: How did the flight of scientists from totalitarian nations affect the outcome of the war? (*Some of these scientists provided the United States with the knowledge to develop the atomic bomb.*)
2. What are some of the countries that scientists left to go to the United States? (*Germany, Italy, Hungary*)

## 3. Check Understanding

**Writing**   Ask students to write a letter from Albert Einstein to President Roosevelt explaining why the president should authorize the development of an atomic bomb.

**Thinking About the Chapter (Hypothesizing)**   Engage the class in a discussion about how Europe's loss was America's gain. Ask students to suggest how things might have turned out if the scientists had remained in Europe.

## Reading Nonfiction

*Analyzing Rhetorical Devices*

Ask students to discuss the question the author asks in the first paragraph. (*Students should understand that she frames her question while making an analogy.*) Point out how the author's question (*both here and in other places in the text*) can shift the reader's perspective of events. Questions like "What would you do?" help readers understand that people had to make decisions that have affected our history, and that people's opinions are an important part of our ongoing history.

## Geography Connections

Make available a map of the world or a globe. Ask students to analyze the statement that the oceans would protect us from danger. Have students study the Atlantic and the Pacific and pay particular attention to the West Coast of the United States and its distance from Japan. How has this sense of protection from the oceans changed?

## More About...

*U.S. Air Force*

When Billy Mitchell served in World War I, air units were part of the U.S. Army Air Service, a branch of the U.S. Army. In 1926, the Air Service was replaced by the Army Air Corps, still a branch of the U.S. Army. After the United States entered World War II, all Army air units were merged into the Army Air Forces (AAF). While the AAF was autonomous under a single commander, it nevertheless was part of the army. Only after World War II, in 1947, did the U.S. Air Force become a separate branch of the military.

# Fighting Wolves

[PAGES 124-126]

### 1 Class Period

### Chapter Summary

Totalitarian aggressors had an unwitting ally in isolationism. As Germany, Italy, and Japan picked off nations one by one, the world's democracies stood immobilized by debate.

### Key Vocabulary

| | | |
|---|---|---|
| Lend-Lease | pacifist | isolationist |
| aircraft carrier | Axis | |

## 1. Connect

Discuss the strategy Germany, Italy, and Japan used—they picked off nations one by one. Suggest that people in other nations may have felt that as long as it wasn't their own country, it wasn't their business.

## 2. Understand

1.  Read pages 124-125 through "...others might do the same." Discuss: Why did totalitarian leaders look down on democratic nations? (*Totalitarian leaders believed that in a democratic nation, debate can make a country slow to act.*) What role did isolationism and pacifism play in the debate? (*Isolationists wanted to stay out of other countries' wars and said the oceans would protect us. Pacifists don't think it is right to fight any war.*)
2.  Read the rest of the chapter. Discuss: What advice did Colonel Billy Mitchell give? (*He said that air power had changed the rules of war and the oceans could not protect us. He urged the United States to build up its air force and build aircraft carriers for the navy.*) How was his advice received? (*He annoyed people and was court-martialed for his ideas.*)

## 3. Check Understanding

**Writing** Ask students to write a letter to the editor of a newspaper reacting to the court-martial of Billy Mitchell.

**Thinking About the Chapter (Comparing and Contrasting)** Ask students to compare the way Einstein's advice was received and the way Mitchell's advice was received. To what do students attribute the difference?

# Pearl Harbor

[PAGES 127-131]

**1 Class Period**

## Chapter Summary

The Japanese planes that rained bombs on Pearl Harbor shattered United States isolationism forever. With American entry into the conflict, the battle against totalitarianism touched nearly every continent.

## Key Vocabulary

blitzkrieg          infamy          fireside chat

## . Connect

Countries in Europe also tried to stay out of the war for as long as they could. Eventually events brought France and England into the war in 1939. In 1941, a Japanese attack brought the United States into the war against Japan, Germany, and Italy.

## 2. Understand

1.  Read pages 127-129 through "In Japan, the military is now supreme." Discuss: What event brought Britain and France into the war? (*The Nazis marched into Poland, and both nations had promised to help Poland if it were attacked.*)
2.  Read the rest of the chapter. Discuss: What attack on the United States took place on December 7, 1941? (*Japanese dive bombers attacked the U.S. naval base at Pearl Harbor in Hawaii.*) What effect did the attack have? (*The United States entered World War II.*)

## 3. Check Understanding

**Writing**  Ask students to write a short news report about the attack on Pearl Harbor.

**Thinking About the Chapter (Recognizing Cause and Effect)**
Discuss with students the effect Japan's bombing of Pearl Harbor had on Americans' feelings of isolationism. Ask students if Japan had made a wise or foolish move in forcing the United States to enter the war.

## Reading Nonfiction

*Analyzing Graphic Aids*

Turn to the map on page 130. First direct students' attention to the inset map. Ask them to find information and missing information. For example: Where was the launching point? (*in the ocean near Hawaii*) What was the departure date from Japan? (*November 2*) The attack date? (*The map doesn't say, but it was Dec. 7*). What does the larger map show? (*the location of U.S. ships in Pearl Harbor*) What do the green lines show? (*battleships*) What is the symbol for oil storage tanks? (*blue dots*)

## Geography Connections

Distribute Resource Page 7 (TG page 108) and have students examine the map of Pearl Harbor on page 130. Instruct students to mark Japan and Hawaii on their outline maps. Then ask students to examine the inset at the upper left of the map on page 130 and add up all the different planes Japan used in the attack. *(354)* Have them determine the number of U.S. ships on Battleship Row. *(8)*

## History Archives

*A History of US Sourcebook*

1. #79, Franklin D. Roosevelt, *Message Asking for War Against Japan* (1941)

2. #80, Franklin D. Roosevelt, *Declaration of War on Germany and Italy* (1941)

## Reading Nonfiction

*Analyzing Word Choice*

Ask students what the author's point of view is toward the technological and code-breaking capabilities of the Americans during the war. (*She thinks they did a great job.*) How do they know? (*by the words she uses to show the accomplishments and her enthusiasm*) Have partners list a noun, for example, *code* or *weapons*, and create a word web showing words and phrases the author uses to describe the item.

## Geography Connections

Distribute Resource Page 4 (TG page 105). As students work their way through these chapters, have them make notes on the outline map of battle locations and what country held which territory during the war.

## Linking Disciplines

*History/Photography*

Point out that photographs as well as words help record history. Have students examine the photos in this chapter and describe what each photo shows.

## Meeting Individual Needs

Encourage advanced students who are interested in military history to read about the German-Soviet invasion of Poland or the German invasion of Russia. Ask students to explain some of their key findings to the class.

# Taking Sides

[ PAGES 132-136 ]

### 1 Class Period

### Chapter Summary

As the war spread, the nations of the world lined up behind two political systems—one democratic, the other totalitarian. The exception was the Soviet Union. An act of treachery by Adolf Hitler forced Soviet dictator Joseph Stalin to join with the Allies—a quirk of history destined to shape the post-World War II era.

### Key Vocabulary

| | |
|---|---|
| Blitz | master race |
| Luftwaffe | *Mein Kampf* |

## 1. Connect

Help students draw up a chart showing the major countries on each side of the war. (*Axis: Germany, Italy, Japan; Allies: United States, Britain, Soviet Union*) Point out that both the United States and Britain had concerns about the Soviet Union.

## 2. Understand

1. Read through the first paragraph on page 134. Discuss: With which side was the Soviet Union allied at the beginning of the war? (*Nazi Germany*) What country did Germany and the Soviet Union invade in 1939? (*Poland*)
2. Read the remainder of the chapter. Discuss: What event made the Soviet Union switch sides? (*Germany invaded Russia.*) Why didn't the Germans succeed? (*They were overcome by a bitter cold Russian winter.*) Why did Great Britain and the United States accept the Soviet Union as an ally? (*They all shared the goal of defeating Hitler.*)

## 3. Check Understanding

**Writing** Ask students to write a news report about the German invasion of Russia.

**Thinking About the Chapter (Sequencing)** Have students put into chronological sequence the events in Chapters 31 and 32.

# World War

[PAGES 137-140]

**1 Class Period**

## Chapter Summary
Fighting a global war forced the United States to mobilize in record time. It also forced the nation to invent and develop technology that would allow troops to fight on the ground, in the air, and on and under the sea.

## Key Vocabulary
| | | |
|---|---|---|
| shrapnel | U-boat | V-1 |
| V-2 | amphibious | cryptography |

## . Connect

Help students recall Colonel Billy Mitchell's concern about building an air force (page 125). The attack on Pearl Harbor showed the importance of air power. Ask students what steps they thought the United States needed to take next.

## 2. Understand

1. Read pages 137-139 ending with "Robert Goddard." Discuss: How did the use of air power change the nature of war? (*It made killing less personal and more mechanical and harmed civilians more heavily.*) How did the war spur new inventions? (*The United States had to develop new means of transportation, new weapons, and new medicines to keep up with and overtake the enemy.*)
2. Read the rest of the chapter. Discuss: How did cryptography play a role in the war? (*Both sides used codes to deliver war plans.*) What advantage did the Allies have in addition to a code? (*They had Navajo soldiers who used their own language to encode messages.*)

## 3. Check Understanding

**Writing**  Ask students to write a plan of action that the United States should take after Pearl Harbor. Plans should detail new weapons and techniques that need to be developed.

**Thinking About the Chapter (Evaluating)**  Engage students in a discussion evaluating the impetus that the war gave to developing new technology. Ask students to determine how much of that technology might also have peacetime applications.

## Geography Connections
Have students use a world map and compare it to the map on page 135. Ask students to locate the countries named on page 137 and then identify other countries (using the names they use today) that were in the war zone.

## Meeting Individual Needs
Encourage advanced students to learn more about codes, to do cryptograms (available in many puzzle magazines), and to try to create their own codes. Some students may want to learn more about modern cryptography.

**JOHNS HOPKINS**
U N I V E R S I T Y

## Analyzing Evil

### 1 Class Period

#### Focus Activity

**1.** Write the following quotations on the chalkboard.
- The only thing necessary for the triumph of evil is for the good men to do nothing.
- He who does not punish evil commands it to be done.
- The opposite of intelligence is not ignorance, it is indifference.…The opposite of life is not death, it is indifference to life and death.
- Those who cannot remember the past are condemned to repeat it.

**2.** Read the quotes aloud. Then divide the class into four teams and assign each team one of the quotes to analyze. Each team is responsible for copying down its assigned quote and discussing it in the context of these questions:
- What is the speaker saying?
- Does the quote suggest when the writer lived?
- Does this quote apply to a specific time in history or to humankind in general?

**3.** Use **Numbered Heads** to have teams report on their analysis of each quote. Then reveal the source of each quote: Edmund Burke (1729-1797), English politician and statesman; Leonardo da Vinci (1452-1519), Italian painter, sculptor, engineer, and architect; Elie Wiesel (1928-), Romanian-born United States writer and Nobel Prize winner; George Santayana (1863-1952), Spanish-born American philosopher, writer, and critic.

#### Student Team Learning Activity/Making Inferences

**1.** Have teams read and discuss Chapter 27.

**2.** Distribute Resource Page 8 (TG page 109) to each student. Explain that teams will use this form to help them analyze one or more of the photographs in Chapter 27.

**3. Circulate and Monitor** Visit each team as they choose a photograph in Chapter 27 to analyze and discuss, using Resource Page 8.

**4.** After the team discussion, ask each student to write answers to the questions on Resource Page 8.

**5. Sharing Information** Use **Numbered Heads** to have teams share observations and insights into the team photograph.

# Summarizing Part 6

## Assessing Part 6
**Part 6 Check-Up**   Use Check-Up 6 (TG page 99) to assess student learning in Part 6.

## Alternate Assessment
Have students write an essay answering one of the following questions that link the big ideas across chapters:

**1. Making Connections**   What was the connection between the rise of totalitarian political systems and the collapse of international justice? (*Totalitarian governments disregard both individual rights and national sovereignty. Encourage students to find examples of injustices committed against individual people or nations in the 1930s.*)

**2. Making Connections**   What was the connection between the Great Depression and the United States' reluctance to enter conflicts overseas? (*Economic turmoil at home made people more receptive to the selfish concerns of isolationism.*)

## Debating the Issues
Use the topic below to stimulate debate.

**Resolved**   That totalitarianism could never take root in the United States. (To address questions raised by the author on page 113, have students debate this topic from the perspective of the late 1930s. Appoint some debaters to cite examples of constitutional guarantees that protect against totalitarianism. Appoint other debaters to find examples of conditions that often fuel the rise of dictators—economic instability, xenophobia, racial prejudice, appeal of demigods such as Father Coughlin, etc. Tell at least one student to question the implications of FDR's election to a third term.)

## Making Ethical Judgments
The following activities ask students to consider issues of ethics.

**1.** Suppose you are in the situation described by the author on page 119. You see a thug beating up an innocent person. What should you do—break up the fight, call the police, or stay out of it? Keeping that personal decision in mind, ask students what action the United States should take when leaders of other nations act like thugs. Should it intervene? Why or why not? (These are highly emotional questions. You might have students answer the first set of questions anonymously on sheets of paper. Read some of these responses aloud. Then explore the responsibility of the United States to stop global thugs of the 1930s, or more recent thugs such as Pol Pot, Saddam Hussein, or the gangsters in Sierra Leone who mutilate people in order to control the diamond market.)

**2.** Imagine that you are a member of Congress in 1939. You must cast your vote on a bill that will allow thousands of Jewish

## Looking Ahead

*Analyzing a Quote*

Read the following selection from a message telegraphed to Washington, D.C., by Winston Churchill:

*[T]he defeat of Germany...will leave Japan exposed to an overwhelming force, whereas the defeat of Japan would by no means bring the World War to an end.*

Upon which region did Churchill urge the United States to concentrate its forces? (*Europe*) If students had been in FDR's shoes, would they have focused on the war in Europe, the war in the Pacific, or given equal attention to both fronts? Compare students' responses with the strategy described in Part 7.

children asylum in the United States. Decide how you will vote. Then write a speech in which you defend your decision. Make sure your speech addresses the question raised by the author on page 121. Does Nazi anti-Semitism have anything to do with the United States? (If students have trouble with this activity, refer them to the quote by Abraham Lincoln on page 120. Then have them write their speech from the point of view of Abe Lincoln, Congressman from Illinois.)

## Projects and Activities

**Analyzing a Quote**    Ask a volunteer to do a dramatic reading of these words from a speech delivered by Adolf Hitler in 1930, at the start of his ascent to power.

*We National Socialists [Fascists] refuse to recognize the treaties concluded over the heads of the German people...and we also propose to fight the war-guilt lie! We shall seek to...revise these [treaties] by diplomatic negotiations, but...if these [methods] fail we shall ignore [the treaties].... The world may call that illegal, but I am answerable to the German people for my actions!*

Review the definition of *nationalism* on page 111. Ask: How does Hitler's speech fit this definition? Considering information in Chapter 26, how do you think Germans reacted to Hitler's speech? Suppose Woodrow Wilson were alive. What warning do you think he might have given to American leaders?

**Delivering Oral Book Reports**    Have interested students read *The Diary of Anne Frank*. Ask them to prepare oral book reports on Anne's tragic experiences under the Nazis.

**Reenacting History**    Have a volunteer read into a tape-recorder the fireside chat on page 131. Then have the rest of the students imagine they are gathered around a radio on February 9, 1942. You might introduce the recording by role-playing the part of a radio announcer. When the fireside chat has ended, ask students these questions: (1) How does FDR say the geography of war has changed? (2) What event proved that Americans could no longer "measure...safety in terms of miles on a map"? (3) What war goals does FDR cite?

**Using Maps**    Have a volunteer use a historical atlas to locate a map showing Hitler's invasion of the Soviet Union. Using an overhead projector, demonstrate the geographic points made by the author on page 135.

**Linking Geography and War**    Divide the class into groups, and have students imagine they have been asked to help the general on page 137-138 plan to invade a Pacific island controlled by the Japanese. Direct student groups to develop a written strategy, including lists of equipment, troop recommendations, necessary maps, and so on. (*Strategies should reflect the geographic obstacles mentioned in Chapter 32.*)

## The Big Ideas

In 1942, war correspondent Ernie Pyle followed U.S. troops into battle. Pyle's front-line reports became some of the most eagerly read news stories of the war. Yet Pyle doubted whether he—or any other reporter—could ever accurately convey the horrors of battle. Pyle confided in one war report from Italy:

> It is hard for you at home to realize what an immense, complicated, sprawling institution...war actually is. As it appears to you in the newspapers, war is a clear-cut matter of landing so many men overseas, moving them from the port to the battlefield, advancing them against the enemy....[W]hat we see...consists only of tired and dirty soldiers who are alive and don't want to die.

Mounting casualty reports soon drove this grim reality into homes across the United States. With more than 15 million men and women enrolled in the military services, the war left few American families untouched. Part 7 explores the changes that this conflict brought to the United States—and to the world.

## Introducing Part 7

### Setting Goals

Introduce Part 7 by reminding students that the United States was now fully in World War II, and we had enemies across both the Atlantic and Pacific Oceans. Ask students how they think we should fight the war? Should we take Churchill's advice? How should we concentrate our efforts?

To set goals for Part 7, tell students they will
- identify what a "two-front war" was and explain how it was fought.
- debate the ethics of the decision to intern Japanese Americans.
- indicate when the war turned in Allied favor.
- describe D-Day and analyze its importance.

### Setting a Context for Reading

**Thinking About the Big Ideas**   You might open Part 7 by reading aloud the statement by Ernie Pyle above. Ask students what Pyle says most newspaper accounts fail to show about war. (*War is more than just the movement of troops.*) To give students a glimpse of the effect of the conflict upon individual soldiers, have volunteers read several paragraphs in the feature on page 160. How does Pyle show that war is more than just "moving troops against an enemy"? (*focuses on the human costs of war; debunks the glory of war*) Given the tragic consequences of war, why did so many American men and women enlist to fight against the Axis? (*Lead students to understand the ideals for which Americans were fighting—justice, liberty, protection of democratic political systems, and so on. Also help students understand that Americans didn't want the United States to be taken*

# PART 7

# Turning the Tide

## [CHAPTERS 33-38]

*over by the Axis and only by fighting against them did the country have a chance of remaining what it is.*)

**Identifying Problem and Solution**   Joy Hakim identifies the problem the United States faced: fighting a war across two oceans at the same time. What are some of the problems in fighting a two-front war? (*You need large numbers of forces and extra equipment. You have to protect the nation from attacks from two directions.*) Tell students the title of Part 7 is "Turning the Tide." Make sure students understand what the expression means and then ask them to suggest ways we found solutions to the problem of a two-front war.

## Setting a Context in Space and Time

**Using Maps**   Refer students to a wall map of the world. Then write *Western Theater (Europe)* and *Pacific Theater (Asia)* on the chalkboard. Ask: Which direction is the Western Theater from the United States? (*east*) To understand how the current use of the terms *West* and *East* crept into our geographic vocabulary, have students read the sidebar on page 141.

Use the wall map or a globe to help students explore the problems involved in fighting a two-ocean war. Have volunteers use the map scale to determine how many miles (or kilometers) separated the West Coast from the Philippines. How many miles (or kilometers) separated the East Coast from France? From a logistical standpoint, what military difficulties did the United States face? Record students' responses for comparison against the information cited in Part 7.

**Using a Chronology**   Assign students to study events listed for the period September 1941 to February 1945 on the Chronology on page 201. Then place on the chalkboard a three-column chart titled *Turning Points of the War* with the headings *Date, Allied Setbacks,* and *Allied Triumphs.* Ask: What year shown on the chart was the bleakest for the Allies? (*1941*) What major setbacks did the United States suffer in the Pacific? (*bombing of Pearl Harbor, loss of Philippines*) What year marked a turning point in the war in the Pacific? (*1942*) What year marked a turning point in the war in Europe? (*1943*)

As an extension, have students add these dates to their class time line. Advise students to use U.S. flags to mark battles that directly involved the United States. (See the time line strategy suggested for Part 6 on TG page 60.)

# A Two-Front War

[PAGES 141-145]

**1 Class Period**

## Chapter Summary

When the attack on Pearl Harbor plunged the United States into World War II, the democratic world teetered on the edge of disaster. The nation faced the daunting task of mobilizing a campaign against well-armed aggressors in regions as far removed as France and the Philippines.

## Key Vocabulary

front          PT boat
theater       hell diver

## 1. Connect

The war was going to be difficult for America and the Allies. Ask students to suggest reasons why our enemies were formidable opponents. (*They had been building up their armaments and fighting for years before the United States entered the war.*).

## 2. Understand

1. Read through the end of the first paragraph on page 143. Ask if students agree with the statement that by 1942, "the Pacific Ocean belonged to the Japanese." (*Most students will agree. Encourage them to support their answers with data from the map on page 144. Students who disagree might cite U.S. victories at Midway and Guadalcanal.*) What problem did the United States face in the Atlantic? (*German U-boats were sinking ships carrying men and supplies to Europe.*)
2. Read the rest of the chapter. Discuss: What human resources did the United States have? (*a president who maintained a confident and courageous manner, outstanding military leaders, determined fighting people*)
3. Map: Distribute Resource Page 7 (TG page 108). Have students use markers to show the areas held by the Japanese in 1942.

## 3. Check Understanding

**Writing** Ask students to write a news analysis for a radio show explaining to the American public why tiny islands in the Pacific Ocean were so important.

**Thinking About the Chapter (Hypothesizing)** Ask students to suppose they were members of the U.S. high command in 1942. How would they divide their forces to fight a two-ocean war? How would they weigh the threats posed by Japan against the threats posed by Germany? You may want to divide the class into groups to devise a wartime strategy for 1942.

## Reading Nonfiction

*Analyzing Point of View*

Although it may appear to be obvious, and the author in no way disguises her viewpoint, it is worth reminding students that this chapter about the Pacific theater is written from an American's point of view. Ask: How does the point of view in this chapter reflect a bias? What would be the interpretation of these events from a Japanese point of view? (*The author is on the American side, so from her point of view events that are "frightening" or "awful" would have been "great" from a Japanese point of view.*)

## Geography Connections

Encourage students to use the map on page 144 to establish general relationships between places. For example, "Korea is west of Japan." Go around the room and ask each student to make a statement describing the spatial relationship of two places. Try to avoid repeats.

## Activities/Johns Hopkins Team Learning

See the Student Team Learning Activity on TG page 79.

Have students examine the three drawings by Miné Okubo on page 148. Then have students write a caption to accompany each drawing.

# Forgetting the Constitution

[PAGES 146-150]

**1 Class Period**

## Chapter Summary

As U.S. troops marched off to battle the forces of totalitarianism, wartime hatreds bred intolerance at home. Anti-Japanese hysteria led President Roosevelt to sign an executive order depriving some 120,000 Japanese Americans of their constitutional rights.

## Key Vocabulary

Nisei    habeas corpus

## 1. Connect

The United States was at war against Japan. What did that mean for American citizens of Japanese descent? Should the Constitution have protected their rights as American citizens? Discuss how other Americans worried about the loyalty of Japanese Americans.

## 2. Understand

1. Read pages 146-148 through "Some people will profit mightily." Discuss: Suppose you were Haruko Obata. What items would you take with you to Tanforan? (*Help students understand how little a person can take by pointing out the small suitcase in the photo on page 146.*)
2. Read the rest of the chapter. Discuss: What constitutional rights were violated by the executive order relocating Japanese Americans? (*Fourth Amendment rights, 14th Amendment rights, right of habeas corpus, etc.*) How did Japanese Americans' actions during the war disprove the charges against them? (*More than 16,000 Nisei served with honor in the Pacific. No Japanese Americans were convicted of spying for Japan.*)

## 3. Assess

**Writing**    Ask students to imagine they have been at Manzanar or Tanforan for about six months and have them write a diary entry for a day, after activities have been organized. Diary entries should describe their activities and their feelings.

**Thinking About the Chapter (Analyzing)**    Engage students in a discussion analyzing how Japanese Americans were treated and why their constitutional rights were ignored. Discuss the concepts that in wartime, governments may usurp powers, racism played a great part, and greed played a part. Also analyze how Japanese Americans may have felt about the actions of Japan against their new country.

# A Hot Island

[PAGES 151-155]

**1 Class Period**

## Chapter Summary

The battle for Guadalcanal shattered Japanese illusions of military superiority. The U.S. victory changed the Pacific conflict into an offensive war aimed at breaking Japan's grip on Asia.

## Key Vocabulary

| | |
|---|---|
| front | anopheles mosquito |
| Seabee | SNAFU |

## 1. Connect

Have students tell how they feel when they are on the defensive about something. (*powerless, having to react to events*) Then ask how their attitudes would shift when they take control of a situation. (*more positive, more powerful*)

## 2. Understand

1. Read pages 151-153, ending with "hiding in the grass behind those jungle trees." Discuss: How did the decision to take Guadalcanal change the nature of the war in the Pacific? (*The United States shifted from a defensive war to an offensive war.*) Why was this tiny island important in the war? (*It was in a strategic location.*)
2. Map: Distribute Resource Page 7 (TG page 108) and ask students to add information from Chapter 35.
3. Read the rest of the chapter. Discuss: Do you think Guadalcanal is a place you'd like to visit? Is it a great place to fight a war? (*Summarize the environmental conditions that make Guadalcanal attractive to tourists but a nightmare to soldiers.*) How did the battle of Guadalcanal change Japanese attitudes toward Americans? (*The Japanese realized they were not unbeatable and that Americans were good fighters.*)

## 3. Check Understanding

**Writing**  Ask students to think of themselves as war correspondents and write a newspaper article about courageous U.S. soldiers and the conditions on Guadalcanal.

**Thinking About the Chapter (Evaluating)**  Remind students that both the Japanese and Americans made serious mistakes on Guadalcanal. Have students make a list of some of the errors each side made and their effects on the battle. Encourage students to cite reasons that the United States finally held the island.

## Reading Nonfiction

*Analyzing Primary and Secondary Sources*

Discuss that the closer in time and place a primary source is to events, the more likely it is the source is credible. Have students read the quotation from James Jones on page 153. Ask students to evaluate whether his description is credible and what information supports their evaluation. (*Below his name it says, "who fought at Guadalcanal." That makes him a person who has been there and is probably credible.*)

## Geography Connections

Have students add information about Guadalcanal to their maps on Resource Page 7 (TG page 108).

## Linking Disciplines

*History/Language Arts*

Review the author's explanation of acronyms on page 154. Then write on the chalkboard these four World War II acronyms: WAAC, WAVE, SPAR, WASP. Explain that all four terms refer to women's military groups—WAAC: Women's Auxiliary Army Corps (Army); WAVE: Women Appointed for Voluntary Emergency Service (Navy); SPAR: Semper Paratus Always Ready Service (Coast Guard); WASP: Women's Airforce Service Pilots (Army Air Forces) Assign groups of students to find out about the role that each of these women's auxiliary units played in the war.

## Reading Nonfiction

*Analyzing Text Features*

Ask students why the author used the bulleted format in pages 156-159. (*To put in chronological order the significant facts of the important events of World War II in 1943.*) Then ask partners to correlate each illustration or photograph with a section of bulleted text.

## Geography Connections

Have students add information on battles for North Africa and Sicily on their maps on Resource Page 1 (TG page 102).

# Axing the Axis

[PAGES 156-160]

**1 Class Period**

### Chapter Summary

In 1943, the war began to turn in the Allies' favor. As cracks appeared in the Axis defense system, German troops braced for an invasion of Fortress Europe.

### Key Vocabulary

| | | |
|---|---|---|
| blitzkrieg | Operation Torch | convoy |
| Red Army | Afrika Korps | bunker |
| Operation Overlord | | Atlantic Wall |

## 1. Connect

While the war against Japan raged in the Pacific, Americans continued fighting alongside the Allies across the Atlantic.

## 2. Understand

1. Read pages 156-157. Discuss: What did Churchill mean by, "We have reached the end of the beginning"? (*Churchill used this play on words to note that the war had finally turned in the Allies' favor.*) What are some examples of this? (*Japan pulled out of Guadalcanal; we began sinking U-boats, we changed our codes and got more ships safely to Europe, and so on.*)

2. Read the rest of the chapter. Discuss: What tactic drove the Axis from North Africa? (*Combined Allied forces successfully attacked the Afrika Korps in a pincer movement.*) Why did the Allies invade Sicily? (*Sicily was strategically located between North Africa and the Italian peninsula.*)

## 3. Assess

**Writing**   Ask students to write a radio news script about the role the U.S. effort at home played in winning the war and to mention some of the work that was done in factories.

**Thinking About the Chapter (Analyzing)**   Encourage a discussion about the importance of information and false information in the conduct of the war. Discuss codes and code breaking and the secrecy surrounding the breaking of codes.

# Going for D-Day

[PAGES 161-165]

## 1 Class Period

## Chapter Summary

On June 6, 1944, Allied troops swept onto the mine-strewn beaches of Normandy. Nazi gunners fired on them from concrete bunkers. But brilliant Allied strategy and acts of individual heroism proved an unbeatable combination. The advance known to history as D-Day unlocked the door to Berlin.

## Key Vocabulary

D-Day        Armada        emplacement

### 1. Connect

All the planning for the invasion of France was about to pay off. Ask students to recall what the Allies had done to help ensure that it was a surprise. (*cleverly misled the Germans about their intentions by planting fake information about a possible invasion*) Point out that several German miscalculations helped the Allied invasion succeed, but nevertheless, it was a hard-fought battle with many lives lost.

### 2. Understand

1. Read pages 161-162. Discuss: What German miscalculations contributed to the success of D-Day? (*They thought the weather conditions were too poor for an invasion and many—including General Rommel—took time off.*) What obstacles did Allied troops face on landing? (*mine-strewn beaches, enemy soldiers in cliff-top bunkers, heavy guns*)
2. Read the rest of the chapter. Discuss: How did the Allies overcome these obstacles? (*by brilliant advance planning and training, use of specially designed equipment, good orchestration of movements, and many individual acts of heroism*) From what countries did the Allied troops come? (*America, Britain, Canada, Free France, Poland*)

### 3. Check Understanding

**Writing** Ask students to use the map on page 164 and write a paragraph telling which nation's forces invaded each beach.

**Thinking About the Chapter (Evaluating)** Remind students of the 1943 quote from Churchill, "We have reached the end of the beginning." Ask students to compare that with the author's last sentence in Chapter 37, "For the Axis, it was the beginning of the end." Encourage students to describe the changes that had taken place between 1943 and D-Day.

## Geography Connections

Have students add information about D-Day to their maps on Resource Page 1 (TG page 102).

## Meeting Individual Needs

Some advanced students might like to find out more about D-Day and re-enact the events using a large map similar to the one on page 164 with tokens of different sorts to represent different troops and equipment.

## Reading Nonfiction

*Analyzing Rhetorical Devices*

Point out that the author invites readers to imagine that they are war correspondents. Discuss with students how this device draws them into events. Then ask individuals to add two sentences to "their" entries for January 27. (*Students should paraphrase the author's note and add a comment of their own.*)

## Linking Disciplines

*History/Photography*

Encourage students to examine the photographs in this chapter. Note that many of them are posed. Ask students to discuss reasons that people want to pose for photographs to commemorate events and mark their importance. Have students compare these photos with those that are not posed and try to make some generalizations about the differences in the nature and purpose of posed and unposed photos.

# A Wartime Diary

[PAGES 166-168]

**1 Class Period**

## Chapter Summary

The rapid-fire events of 1945 made it clear that the Axis had no chance of winning the war. Yet neither Germany nor Japan would surrender. Instead they retreated into their home countries to wage a desperate fight to the finish.

## Key Vocabulary

| | |
|---|---|
| Battle of the Bulge | Yalta |
| Big Three | United Nations |

### 1. Connect

Neither the Germans nor Japanese were willing to give up even though they no longer had any hope of winning the war. Ask students what they think were the consequences of prolonging the war. (*more suffering and loss of life*)

### 2. Understand

1. Read pages 166-167, through events of February 1. Discuss: Why was the Battle of the Bulge an important turning point in Europe? (*It was Hitler's last gamble on the western front.*)
2. Read the rest of the chapter. Discuss: What took place at Yalta? (*The Big Three—Roosevelt, Churchill, and Stalin—planned the final battles of the war, mapped out plans for peace, and initiated the creation of the United Nations.*) What was happening in the Pacific while the Allies were moving on Germany? (*The Marines landed on Iwo Jima and General MacArthur returned to retake the Philippines.*)

### 3. Check Understanding

**Writing** Ask students to write a newspaper editorial calling for the surrender of either Germany or Japan and explaining the reasons for their opinion.

**Thinking About the Chapter (Evaluating)** Britain and America were allied with the Soviet Union in order to fight a common enemy, but now the war was winding down. Ask students to discuss the suggestion in the cartoon on page 167 that Stalin had secret plans. What might the secret plans be? Discuss the problem of working with an untrustworthy ally.

## Exploring World War II

## Several Class Periods

### Focus Activity

**1.** Divide the class into teams. Allow teams one or two minutes to **Brainstorm** what they know about World War II, quickly listing people, places, and events.

**2.** Use **Numbered Heads** to have teams share a few of their responses with the class.

### Student Team Learning Activity/Developing a Topic to Investigate

**1.** Explain to the class that they will be investigating questions and topics about World War II. Each team will choose a topic. Topics might include a famous battle or general, less-well-known but fascinating topics such as Navajo code talkers or women war photographers, or questions such as, Why did the Allies wait until 1944 to invade Europe?

**2.** Write the following headings on the chalkboard for teams to use in creating a form describing a topic for your approval.

- Team Names
- Topic or Question
- Questions We Need to Answer About Our Topic (consider who, what, when, where, why, and how)

**3.** To help teams identify a topic or question to investigate further, have them skim Chapters 31-39, 42, and 44. Then ask teams to complete their forms and have you initial them. (At this point, *Questions We Need to Answer About Our Topic* does not need to be completed.)

**4. Circulate and Monitor** Visit teams as they explore the chapters and choose their topics and questions. If necessary, prompt students in the process of browsing the chapters and choosing a topic to investigate. Guide students in identifying topics that are neither too narrow nor too broad.

**5.** Once teams have your approval, have them complete the form with a list of questions to guide further investigation.

**6.** Students will make use of the information they gather in this activity in Part 8.

# Summarizing Part 7

## Assessing Part 7

**Part 7 Check-Up**    Use Check-Up 7 (TG page 100) to assess student learning in Part 7.

## Alternate Assessment

**1. Making Connections**    What was the link between Pearl Harbor and the violation of rights of Japanese Americans? *(Answers will vary. Lead students to understand that a so-called wartime emergency was used as an excuse to deprive citizens of their rights on purely racial grounds, without any proof—or even hint—of treasonous behavior.)*

**2. Making Connections**    What was the link between United States factories and Allied victories in Europe and Asia? *(United States factories turned out the equipment and weapons needed to defeat the Axis powers.)*

## Debating the Issues

Use the topic below to stimulate debate.

**Resolved**    That the fourth-term election of Franklin Roosevelt presented a clear and present danger to our constitutional system. (Appoint some students to challenge the increased power of the presidency and the threat that it presents to the system of checks and balances. Have others defend the right of the people to elect a president as often as they want—especially in time of crisis. For added interest, ask one student to speak for George Washington, the president who started the two-term tradition.)

## Making Ethical Judgments

The following activities ask students to consider issues of ethics.

**1.** Suppose you are a Nisei living in an internment camp such as Manzanar. You've just learned that the United States is enlisting Nisei for service in the Pacific. Will you sign up? Why or why not? (You might suggest that students write a dialogue in which two Nisei weigh the pros and cons of service.)

**2.** You are in charge of a blood bank and have been told that blood from black and white donors must be segregated. You don't believe that is necessary. Would you comply with orders to segregate blood? Would you refuse to give blood to a person because there was no blood of the same race?

## Projects and Activities

**Using Historical Imagination**    Have students review the story of William (Billy) Mitchell in Chapter 29. Then challenge them to create a skit in which Mitchell appeals his court-martial for outspoken criticism of the military's reluctance to develop U.S. air power. Mitchell should begin his appeal with a list of World War II battles in which air power played a significant role.

**Designing a Commemorative Stamp**    Ask a volunteer to read aloud the profile of Charles R. Drew on page 142. Then assign groups of students to design a commemorative postage stamp honoring Drew's accomplishments. (Bring in other commemorative stamps released by the U.S. Postal Service as models.)

**Writing a Rebuttal**    Distribute copies of this statement by General John DeWitt, the official in charge of relocation.

> *It makes no difference whether a Japanese is theoretically a citizen. He is still a Japanese. Giving him a scrap of paper won't change him.*

Assign students to write a rebuttal of this statement from a Nisei serving in the "Go for Broke" 442nd Infantry Division, one of the most highly decorated units in the war.

**Preparing Mock Radio Reports**    Chapter 36 highlights some of the major news events of 1943. Assign groups of students to present each of these events in the form of special radio broadcasts to the nation. You might repeat this strategy with Chapter 38, which highlights some of the major events in 1945. (An alternative approach is to present these events in the form of newspaper headlines to be posted in chronological order on the bulletin board.)

**Preparing a Citation**    As the note on acronyms for Chapter 35 explains, there were a variety of women in the military or assisting the military. Assign groups of students to find out about the role that each of these women's auxiliary units played in the war, and have each group write a citation to honor that group.

**Delivering a Speech**    In June 1994, people in the United States and Europe celebrated the 50th anniversary of D-Day. Ask students to prepare speeches that leaders of the Allied nations might have delivered on this historic occasion.

## Looking Ahead

*Making Inferences*

On August 6, 1945, President Truman issued this warning:

> *We are now prepared to obliterate...every productive enterprise the Japanese have....if they do not now accept our terms they may expect a rain of ruin from the air, the like of which has never been seen on this earth.*

Remind students that Part 7 ends in March 1945. What do the speaker's identity and the content of the quote tell them about changes that took place between March and August? What do students think the phrase "rain of ruin" refers to? Then write the title of Part 8, "Redefining War and Peace," on the chalkboard. Use this title to introduce the impact of the atomic bomb.

# PART 8

## Redefining War and Peace

### [CHAPTERS 39-45]

## The Big Ideas

On September 2, 1945, General Douglas MacArthur addressed the American people from aboard a ship anchored in Tokyo Bay. MacArthur said:

*Today the guns are silent. A great tragedy has ended. A great victory has been won.…[However,] the lesson of victory itself brings with it profound concern.…The destructiveness of war potential, through progressive advances in scientific discovery, has in fact now reached a point which revises the traditional concept of war.*

Use of the atomic bomb had helped ensure the triumph of democratic political systems. But it also ensured that future conflicts would be even more deadly than the one ended by the bomb. Part 8 traces the closing days of World War II and the awesome responsibility assumed by the United States as the guardian of international justice.

## Introducing Part 8

### Setting Goals

Refer to the title of Part 8—"Redefining War and Peace." Read General MacArthur's statement to the class. What "profound concern" does he say victory has brought? *(a change in the traditional concept of war because of greater destructive potential through advances in science)*

To set goals for Part 8, tell students that they will
- describe the sudden change that took place after FDR's death.
- explain how the war in Europe ended and why the war against Japan continued.
- evaluate what Truman had to consider in deciding whether to use the atomic bomb.
- debate what is meant by "redefining war and peace."

### Setting a Context for Reading

**Thinking About the Big Ideas**   To open Part 8, you might refer students to the newspaper headline on page 173. What changes have taken place in the United States? *(death of Roosevelt; inauguration of Truman)* Why do such transfers of power go smoothly in our political system? *(because the Constitution provides for presidential succession)* Ask students to speculate on the decisions Truman will face at the end of the war. List student predictions on the chalkboard for comparison as they read Part 8.

**Drawing Conclusions**   Alert students that they will be drawing conclusions about various events toward the end of World War II. Why didn't the Germans and Japanese surrender when their cause was hopeless? Was Truman prepared to be president? Did he live up to the demands of that role?

## Setting a Context in Space and Time

**Linking Geography and War**   Refer students to the map on page 181. Recall the conduct of World War I. How had military technology changed since then? (*The use of airplanes increased; aircraft carriers and the atomic bomb were developed.*) Based on this map and the map on page 133, what geographic factors might have influenced these changes? (*logistics of a two-ocean war, Japan's island location, and so on*)

Write *radioactive fallout* on the chalkboard. Ask students to define or look up the meaning of this term. (*the descent to earth of radioactive particles after an atomic or nuclear explosion*) What nations do students think might be most affected by the fallout carried by wind currents out of Japan? (*Use students' answers to underscore reasons the atomic bomb soon became an international issue.*)

**Forming Chronological Generalizations**   Tell students that the six chapters in Part 8 cover only a small time period—April-August 1945. Ask students to study the events listed for this period in the Chronology on pages 200-201. Then have students write generalizations about why these months were so important to world history.

## Reading Nonfiction

*Analyzing Rhetorical Devices*

Point out that the word *madmen* in the first sentence of the chapter is an example of a loaded word, or a word that has a strong connotation and is used to sway the reader's opinion. Have partners find other loaded words in the chapter that describe the Nazis (*malignant, Kill their own people, war lords*). Then have them write a sentence or two explaining the generally held view of the Nazis.

## Activities/Johns Hopkins Team Learning

See the Student Team Learning Activity on TG page 90.

## More About...

*Health Reports on Presidents*

The American people today get regular health reports on the president, vice president, and other high government officials. In the past, matters of presidents' health were kept secret. Presidents received medical attention away from the public eye, and doctors did not divulge information about the health of their presidential patients. Thus, although Roosevelt's doctors knew his health was failing as he ran for a fourth term, the American public did not have this information when they went to vote.

## Meeting Individual Needs

Have a group of advanced students work together as an "advisory panel" to the newly sworn-in President Truman. Have the panel make a list of suggestions for ending the war, making a just peace, and leading the country.

# April in Georgia
[PAGES 169-171]

# President HST
[PAGES 172-173]

**1 Class Period**

## Chapter Summary

As Roosevelt entered his fourth term, he began mapping out plans for peace. But FDR never saw his ideas tested. His death thrust the job of ending the war and designing a peace into the lap of Harry Truman.

## Key Vocabulary

Atlantic Charter          self-determination          retribution

## 1. Connect

It is April 1945. Ask students how long FDR has served as president. (*since March 1933, just over 12 years*) Discuss the two major crises he had led the nation through—the Great Depression and World War II. Point out that the difficult job of making the peace still lay ahead.

## 2. Understand

1. Read Chapter 39. Discuss: Why do you think the Axis leaders are not ending the war? (*Possible answers are they care more about themselves or their countries' honor than about their people; they are worried about harsh peace terms.*) What was FDR's goal for the end of the war? (*He wanted an end to all wars and better ways of settling differences between governments.*)
2. Read Chapter 40. Discuss: What personal characteristics did Truman have? What experience did he have? (*Students should base their answers on the first paragraph on page 173.*) What did Eleanor Roosevelt mean when she told Truman, "You are the one in trouble now"? (*Truman now had to face the pressures of ending the war, finding a just peace, leading the country, and leading the world.*)

## 3. Check Understanding

**Writing**   Ask students to write an obituary for FDR.

**Thinking About the Chapter (Analyzing)**   Discuss the reasons given for Truman having been chosen as FDR's running mate. Ask students whether the reasons are a good way of choosing someone who may end up serving as president. Would Truman have been chosen if Democratic party leaders had known that FDR was going to die soon? Can bad reasons still lead to a good decision?

# A Final Journey

[PAGES 174-177]

**1 Class Period**

## Chapter Summary

People measured Franklin Delano Roosevelt by the hope that he inspired. His death triggered a mass outpouring of grief rivaled only by the tear-filled tribute paid to another wartime president—Abraham Lincoln.

## . Connect

Ask students to explain this statement: Americans needed to mourn their dead president before they turned to a new president for leadership. (*FDR had been the people's leader through hard times; people were sad and could not easily switch loyalties to a relatively unknown person.*)

## Understand

1. Read pages 174-175. Discuss: What did Roosevelt and Lincoln have in common? (*Both restored people's faith during difficult times, both saw the nation through destructive wars; both inspired controversy as well as deep love among the people; both hoped for a just peace after the war; both died suddenly in office.*)
2. Read the rest of the chapter. Discuss: What flaws did FDR have as a leader? (*He could be devious, sometimes told stories to look good; seemed to agree with people to their face when he really disagreed.*) What were FDR's accomplishments? (*Students' answers should reflect the ideas in the topic sentences of each bulleted paragraph on these two pages.*)

## Check Understanding

**Writing**  Ask students to select one of the quotations on pages 176-177 and write a poem or paragraph based on the quotation explaining its significance.

**Thinking About the Chapter (Analyzing)**  Discuss the reasons FDR was loved and hated. Refer to this chapter and others, especially Chapter 25. Encourage students to identify the groups of people who were most likely to love him and those who were most likely to hate him.

## Linking Disciplines

*History/Art*

Ask students to create a work of art in response to the death of FDR. Their work can be realistic or abstract, but it should convey the mood of the nation.

## Geography Connections

Have students refer to their copies of Resource Page 4 (TG page 105). Ask them to mark the events and dates in this chapter on their maps.

## Meeting Individual Needs

Have advanced students stage a reenactment of the event mentioned for May 7—German military leaders surrender to General Eisenhower.

# Day by Day

[PAGES 178-181]

## 1 Class Period

## Chapter Summary

Within a month of Roosevelt's death, Nazi Germany surrendered unconditionally. But Japanese warlords refused to consider terms of peace. Their resistance pushed Truman closer and closer to the use of a top-secret superweapon destined to reshape world history.

## Key Vocabulary

VE Day          kamikaze          Third Reich

### 1. Connect

Have students consider the title of the chapter and comment on what it suggests. (*a diary, steady but slow advances, frustrating slowness, progress*)

### 2. Understand

1. Read pages 178-180 through the entry for May 7. Discuss: What did Nazi concentration camps reveal to the world about the evils of totalitarianism? (*the Nazi system's total disregard of even the most basic human rights*) What was VE Day? (*Victory in Europe day, the day the war in Europe was over*)

2. Read the rest of the chapter. Discuss: Did VE Day mark the end of World War II? (*No, the war against Japan continued.*) What action by the Japanese warlords in July revealed their continuation of totalitarianism? (*They refused to surrender despite the suffering of millions of their people. They arrested Japanese who talked about surrender.*)

### 3. Check Understanding

**Writing**   Ask students to write a letter to Joseph Stalin arguing against (or for) reparations. Students should base their arguments on historical precedent.

**Thinking About the Chapter (Evaluating)**   Begin a discussion of the actions the Allies were taking to end the war in the Pacific. Discuss reasons why the actions were not taking effect. Note the inclusion of China's leader Chiang Kai-shek in the conference at Potsdam. Discuss the suggestion of a "new and powerful weapon."

# A Little Boy

[PAGES 182-185]

**1 Class Period**

## Chapter Summary

In one of the most agonizing—and hotly debated—decisions in U.S. history, President Truman unleashed the atomic bomb against Japan. The mushroom cloud that rose above Hiroshima became the symbol of the atomic age.

## Key Vocabulary

| | | |
|---|---|---|
| superfortress | shock wave | thermal rays |
| atomic bomb | mushroom cloud | |

## 1. Connect

Explain to students that President Truman took office on April 8, but it wasn't until April 24 that he received a detailed briefing on the top-secret atomic bomb. Ask students whom a president can call on for help in making a decision such as this one. (*experts such as scientists and soldiers; political advisors*)

## 2. Understand

1. Read pages 182-183. Discuss: What factors influenced Truman's decision to use the atomic bomb against Japan? (*Japan's refusal to surrender, the possibility of more years of war and high casualties if the United States were to invade Japan*)

2. Read the rest of the chapter. Discuss: Did the United States try to warn the Japanese? (*Yes, but the warning wasn't taken seriously.*) What damage did the atomic bomb inflict on Hiroshima? (*Buildings were destroyed and thermal rays burned people; Japan's 2nd Army was destroyed; 78,000 people died and another 100,000 were injured. Students may add other information from the photos.*)

## 3. Check Understanding

**Writing** Ask students to write one argument for using Little Boy and one argument against it.

**Thinking About the Chapter (Analyzing)** Reread aloud the last sentence of the chapter, "The atomic age has begun." Initiate a class discussion of what the implications were for the world.

## Geography Connections

Distribute Resource Page 7 (TG page 108). Have students use the outline maps to compare the map on page 183 with the map on page 144. Ask students to identify some areas that had been under Japanese control in 1942 and that were now under U.S. control. Help students understand how regaining small islands in the Pacific allowed America to bomb Japan.

## Meeting Individual Needs

Encourage students interested in science to research both the positive and negative applications of atomic or nuclear energy, the long-lasting effects of exposure to radiation, and current international efforts to limit nuclear weapons while encouraging safer nuclear plants.

## Reading Nonfiction

*Analyzing Rhetorical Devices*

Reread the author's question on page 186, "Has this war driven sane people to act insanely?" This is a double-edged rhetorical question. Who was acting insanely: the Americans who dropped the second atomic bomb, or the Japanese for not surrendering after the first atomic bomb was dropped?

## Linking Disciplines

*History/Photography*

Encourage students to compare and contrast the photographs in this chapter—the two photos of American reactions and the photos involving the Japanese officials.

# Peace

[ PAGES 186-187 ]

**1 Class Period**

## Chapter Summary

On August 15, 1945, Emperor Hirohito said the time had come to "bear the unbearable." With peace or atomic rain as Japan's only choices, he chose peace.

## Key Vocabulary

Potsdam Declaration

## 1. Connect

Discuss with students why people thought the atomic bomb that destroyed Hiroshima would lead the warlords to surrender. (*fear that more atomic bombs would be dropped*) Explain that it became apparent that they would not surrender under any circumstances.

## 2. Understand

1. Read page 186. Discuss: What attacks against Japan followed the Hiroshima atomic bomb? (*The Russians entered the war and attacked Japan's army in Manchuria and Korea. The United States dropped a second atomic bomb on Nagasaki.*) Who in Japan continued to oppose surrender, and who finally decided to surrender? (*The warlords opposed surrender; Emperor Hirohito ordered the surrender, provided he remained head of state.*)
2. Read page 187. Discuss: How did some Japanese army officers react to the surrender? (*They broke into the imperial palace and eventually committed suicide.*) Who told the Japanese people to accept peace? (*Emperor Hirohito*)

## 3. Check Understanding

**Writing**   Ask students to write a news broadcast for U.S. radio announcing VJ (Victory in Japan) Day.

**Thinking About the Chapter (Identifying Point of View)**
Assign teams of students to represent different American citizens, such as veterans who fought the Japanese, citizens who lost loved ones in the war, historians, and diplomats. Hold a discussion in which the different groups comment on how they think Japan should be treated after the war. Each group should support its position.

# Picturing History

[PAGES 188-199]

**1 Class Period**

### Chapter Summary

This chapter looks at the art that developed in America during the period covered in this text. Much of the art departs from the tradition of the first decades of the 20th century. Many of the works were rejected at first by the art establishment.

### Key Vocabulary

catalyst traditionalist modernist
realist  avant-garde

## . Connect

Ask students to discuss the kinds of artwork they like. Point out that many art styles we admire today were rejected as inferior when they first appeared. Encourage students to enjoy this chapter. You may also want to encourage students to compare changes taking place in American art with changes in music described in Chapter 11.

## 2. Understand

1. Divide the class into teams to read and discuss each section of the chapter.
2. Have the teams choose one work of art from each section to present to the class, explaining its significance then and now.

## 3. Check Understanding

**Writing** Ask students to write a paragraph or a poem using one of the paintings as inspiration.

**Thinking About the Chapter (Synthesizing)** Read aloud the remark made by Sir Caspar Purdon Clarke of the Metropolitan Museum of Art in New York City (page 188): "There is a state of unrest all over the world in art as in all other things." Ask students to give examples of unrest in the world during the 20th century and unrest in art as presented in this chapter.

## Reading Nonfiction

*Analyzing Point of View*

Refer students to pages 198-199. Ask students to find the sentence that defines the author's point of view about the WPA. (*"The most creative idea our government…"*) Then ask partners to list the facts, evidence, and anecdotes the author gives to support her point of view.

## Linking Disciplines

*History/Art*

Encourage students to create a piece of art related to an event in Book Nine.

## Radio Broadcasts

## 1 Class Period

### Focus Activity

Conduct a class survey to determine how many students listen to the radio "frequently," "sometimes," "very rarely," or "never." Chart the results on the chalkboard. Then ask the same question about television. Discuss with students the importance of radio before televisions were widely available.

### Student Team Learning Activity/Presenting Radio Broadcasts

**1.** Divide the class into teams of five students. Explain that they will prepare and present radio broadcasts based on the work that they did for the Student Team Learning Activity in Part 7 (TG page 79). Review the following radio broadcast guidelines with students.

- Time: Each team has up to ten minutes (maximum two minutes per team member) to present its radio broadcast. Adherence to time limits will be strictly enforced as in a real radio (or television) broadcast.
- Format: Each team member is a reporter. One or more team members act as the anchorperson.
- Notes: Student may use notes or their own written scripts to guide their presentations.
- Evaluation: When their team is not presenting, each student will write a one-sentence summary of each presentation and an evaluation.

**2.** Play some recorded music from the 1940s to set the mood.

**3.** Have students use the topics and questions they researched in Part 7 to prepare their material for a broadcast.

**4. Circulate and Monitor** Visit each team and offer guidance in content, planning, and timing for the broadcast. Encourage teams to rehearse with a timer so they can make sure each team member's presentation is no more than two minutes long.

**5.** Each team presents its radio broadcast. Use a timer to keep students within their two-minute limit and the team within its ten-minute limit.

**6.** Invite the audience to evaluate each presentation carefully, looking at Preparation, Organization, Use of Research, and Delivery, and giving each category a rank of Poor, Fair, Good, or Excellent.

# Summarizing Part 8

## Assessing Part 8

**Part 8 Check-Up**   Use Check-Up 8 (TG page 101) to assess student learning in Part 8.

## Alternate Assessment

Ask students to create an annotated time line of the events that ended World War II.

**Making Connections**   At his fourth inauguration, President Roosevelt said, "We have learned to be citizens of this world." What lessons in global citizenship did World War II teach Americans? (*Lead students to link the rise of totalitarianism to the end of U.S. isolationism. Also explore how wartime atrocities such as the Nazi concentration camps taught Americans to empathize with injustices suffered by people beyond U.S. borders.*)

## Debating the Issues

Use the topic below to stimulate debate.

**Resolved**   That the United States acted correctly in using the atomic bomb against Japan. (This is still a hotly debated topic. Advise students to keep the debate within the framework of the time. To stimulate debate, you might have Harry Truman head the "pro" team. You might have Albert Einstein, who later questioned his decision to promote the bomb, head the "con" team. For more on Einstein, refer students to Chapter 28.)

## Making Ethical Judgments

The following activities ask students to consider issues of ethics.

**1.** Put yourself in the shoes of President Roosevelt and President Truman. Would you allow a dictator like Joseph Stalin to take part in setting the terms of peace? (Both presidents grappled with this question. The Soviets paid a high price to defeat the Germans. Disregarding their role might have provided fuel for a future war. However, as Hitler proved, appeasement could also lead to war. Use this question to explore whether the United States had a moral responsibility to stop aggression in the postwar world. You might save students' responses for review during the discussion of the Cold War in Book Ten.)

**2.** Imagine that you are President Roosevelt. You have led the nation through the Great Depression and now you are leading it through the end stages of World War II. You know that your health is failing, but you believe that you are the best person to lead the nation. Should you run for a fourth term? (Some students may believe that FDR had earned the right to see the war through to its finish. Others may believe he was deceiving voters by not being candid about his health.)

## Projects and Activities

**Conducting a Poll**   Have students prepare a list of past presidents to distribute to U.S. history classes in your school system.

## Looking Ahead

*Forming Hypotheses*

On March 5, 1946, Winston Churchill delivered a famous speech in Fulton, Missouri. In it he stated:

*A shadow has fallen upon the scenes so lately lighted by Allied victory....From Stettin in the Baltic to Trieste in the Adriatic, an iron curtain has descended across the continent. Behind that line lie all the capitals of the ancient states of central Europe....*

Have students locate on a map of the world the line of what Churchill called the "iron curtain." What nation do they think lowered the iron curtain? (*Soviet Union*) What evidence supports their answer? What conflicts or power struggles can students predict for the post-war era?

At the top of the list, tell students to write the following directions: *Indicate your choice for the five greatest presidents in our history. Mark your first choice with a 1, your second choice with a 2, and so on.* Direct students to tally the results. Then have them compare the findings with the poll reported on page 175. Where does President Roosevelt rank today? Is he included on most of the lists? If so, where does he place?

**Using Historical Imagination**    Tell students to imagine they are President Roosevelt. He suspects that his health is failing. So he writes a letter for Harry Truman to read upon his death. The letter begins, "Dear Harry, If you are reading this letter, you are now the president of the United States." Challenge students to complete the letter, offering advice that FDR might give to Truman about ending World War II.

**Turning Pictures into Words**    Refer students to the photo at the bottom of page 187. Tell them to imagine they are reporters covering the announcement of VJ Day in New York City. Instruct students to prepare mock radio reports describing the scene for audiences outside of New York City. (Remind students to create a visual picture through the use of descriptive, colorful language and vivid details.)

**Designing a Book Cover**    Ask students to imagine that Joy Hakim has decided to bind Chapters 26-44 into a separate volume on World War II. Assign groups of students to design a cover for the new book.

Use the following questions to help students pull together some of the major concepts and themes covered in this book. Note: You may want to assign these as essay questions for assessment.

# SYNTHESIZING THE BIG IDEAS IN BOOK NINE

**1.** History is filled with "what ifs." For example: What if President Wilson had persuaded the Allies and the U.S. Congress to follow his Fourteen Points? How might later events have been different? (*Some of the German bitterness about the Versailles Treaty might have been averted, providing Hitler with less ammunition for his rise to power. Also, the United States might have made the League of Nations a stronger force for peace.*)

**2.** A U.S. historian has written: "*Few decades in American history are as sharply separated from the events that preceded and followed them as the decade of the 1920s.*" Ask: Why do you think the historian made this statement? Do you agree or disagree? Why? (*The decade preceding the 1920s was marked by the crusades of progressivism and World War I. The decade after it was marked by economic crisis and growing international threats. The 1920s seemed to be a time of isolationism, normalcy, and materialism. Students should give their own reasons for agreeing or disagreeing.*)

**3.** Shortly after this country's founding, George Washington said, "The government of the United States…gives to bigotry no sanction, to persecution no assistance." Do you think that in the years covered by Book Nine the United States lived up to Washington's assertion? What specific examples of justice or injustice support your opinion? (*Students may cite such factors as the Red Scare, the refusal to grant asylum to European Jews, and the internment of Japanese Americans to show flaws existed.*)

**4.** "The American political system works best in times of crisis." Do you agree or disagree with this statement, based on the evidence from Book Nine? (*Students who agree might cite rapid mobilization during two world wars and the array of FDR's new programs to fight the Depression. Those who disagree might cite the federal government's paralysis during Hoover's term and government's failure to protect individual liberties during the Red Scare and the Japanese internment.*)

**5.** Which do you think posed the greater threat to the United States: the Great Depression or World War II? Explain your answer. (*Both threatened the nation's political system, one from within and one from without, each producing different kinds of conflict and threat.*)

**6.** In Book Nine, the author asks, "Did we learn anything from the history of the first half of the 20th century?" How would you answer her question? (*This question can spark a free-flowing discussion in which each of the Big Ideas for Book Nine— change, conflict, political systems, and justice— is explored to determine how events involving them in the first half of the past century touch our lives today.*)

# CHECK-UP 1

*Answering the following questions will help you understand and remember what you have read in Chapters 1-3. Write your answers on a separate sheet of paper.*

1. The people listed below played important roles in events described in Chapters 1 to 3. Tell who each person was and what role he played in this period in our history.
   a. Woodrow Wilson
   b. Georges Clemenceau
   c. Oliver Wendell Holmes, Jr.
   d. Abraham Flexner

2. Explain the relationship of Washington, D.C., and Versailles to the League of Nations.

3. Define each of these terms. Then explain its significance to the events of the time.
   a. neutral
   b. self-determination
   c. isolation
   d. espionage
   e. sedition
   f. pandemic

4. Complete the following sentence as it might have been written by President Woodrow Wilson: With the defeat of the Central Powers, the United States had won the chance to _____.

5. History is full of "what ifs." They help you assess the impact of a person or event. How might these "what ifs" have changed history?
   a. What if Germany had made every effort to avoid sinking U.S. ships?
   b. What if President Wilson had asked leading Republican senators to accompany him to Paris for the peace conference?

6. How did the peace goals of President Wilson differ from those of the leaders of the Big Four nations?

7. Which of Wilson's Fourteen Points do you think was most important? Write a brief argument that Wilson might have used at the peace conference in support of that point.

8. The influenza outbreak claimed five times as many American lives as did World War I. Which event do you think had the greater impact on the nation? Explain your answer,

9. Who do you think would have most favored the idea of a return to normalcy in 1919: an African American sharecropper in Alabama, a woman worker in a sweatshop on the Lower East Side of New York City, a returning soldier who had been a worker in a Ford automobile factory before the war? Explain your answer.

10. **Thinking About the Big Ideas** How did political conflict in the United States reduce the chances for an enduring end to conflicts between nations after World War I?

# CHECK-UP 2

*Answering the following questions will help you understand and remember what you have read in Chapters 4-8. Write your answers on a separate sheet of paper.*

1. The people listed below played important roles in events described in Chapters 4-8. Identify each person and tell how the pair was connected.
   a. Alice Paul, Carrie Chapman Catt
   b. William Jennings Bryan, Clarence Darrow
   c. Warren G. Harding, Calvin Coolidge
   d. Niccola Sacco, Bartolomeo Vanzetti

2. Identify each of the places below and explain its importance to the events described in Chapters 4-8.
   a. Yoncalla, Oregon
   b. Teapot Dome, Wyoming
   c. Harlem, New York City
   d. Dayton, Tennessee

3. Define each of the following terms and explain its importance to the events described in Chapters 4-8.
   a. prohibition
   b. suffragist
   c. bootlegger
   d. anarchist
   e. flapper

4. Prohibition was sometimes called "the noble experiment." Explain why you think it got that name and whether you believe it was deserved.

5. Imagine that you are a suffragist picketing the White House in 1917. Write a letter to President Wilson explaining why you are doing so.

6. Write a memorandum that A. Mitchell Palmer might have sent to President Wilson explaining the threat he believed communists and anarchists posed to the nation and what he planned to do about it.

7. Imagine that you are a voter in the 1920s. Explain why you would or would not have supported Warren G. Harding if he had lived to run for reelection.

8. "The Roaring Twenties were a wonderful time for Americans." Briefly explain why you agree or disagree with that statement.

9. **Thinking About the Big Ideas** What is the connection between the banning of the sale of alcohol and the granting of the vote to women?

10. **Thinking About the Big Ideas** Do the years discussed in Chapters 4-8 represent an advance or a setback for the rights of Americans guaranteed under the First Amendment to the Constitution?

# CHECK-UP 3

*Answering the following questions will help you understand and remember what you have read in Chapters 9-14. Write your answers on a separate sheet of paper.*

1. The people listed below were important figures during the years discussed in Chapters 9-14. Identify each person and tell why he or she was well known during that period.
   a. Babe Ruth
   b. Babe Didrikson Zaharias
   c. Jesse Owens
   d. Louis Armstrong
   e. Duke Ellington
   f. Robert H. Goddard
   g. Charles A. Lindbergh, Jr.

2. Explain the importance of New Orleans, Louisiana, and Hollywood, California, to entertainment in the United States during the period discussed in Chapters 9-14.

3. Define each of these terms. Then explain how each was related to some person or event during the period discussed in Chapters 9-14.
   a. southpaw
   b. barnstorm
   c. jazz
   d. improvisation
   e. rocket

4. Write the inscription that might have appeared on a plaque honoring Babe Ruth as Outstanding Baseball Player of the 1920s.

5. Write a radio advertisement that might have been used to attract customers to a game by teams in the Negro Leagues.

6. Jazz has been called "the only original American art form." Write a brief paragraph explaining why you agree or disagree with that statement.

7. Write a short letter that Charles Lindbergh might have sent to Daniel Guggenheim asking for aid for Robert H. Goddard.

8. Draw a cartoon that might have appeared in a newspaper of the 1920s commenting on Charles Lindbergh's achievement.

9. The 1920s were a time of "ballyhoo," of insignificant events blown out of proportion to their true importance. Pick one event from Chapters 9-14 and explain why you think it is an example of ballyhoo.

10. **Thinking About the Big Ideas** Which of the people discussed in Chapters 9-14 do you think produced the most lasting change in some aspect of American life? Explain your choice.

# CHECK-UP 4

*Answering the following questions will help you understand and remember what you have read in Chapters 15-18. Write your answers on a separate sheet of paper.*

1. The people listed below took part in events described in Chapters 15-18. Identify each person and explain his role in those events.
   a. Al Smith
   b. Herbert Hoover
   c. Douglas MacArthur
   d. Franklin D. Roosevelt

2. Identify each of the places below and explain its importance in events of the Great Depression.
   a. New York City
   b. Washington, D.C.
   c. Great Plains

3. Define each of the following terms and explain its importance to the events described in Chapters 15-18.
   a. stock
   b. law of supply and demand
   c. bull market
   d. panic
   e. depression
   f. Hooverville
   g. evicted
   h. voluntarism

4. About the 1928 presidential campaign someone wrote: "There is opposition to Smith which is…inspired by the feeling that the clamorous life of the city should not be acknowledged as the American ideal." Briefly explain this statement and the effect that feelings like this had on the campaign and the election.

5. Imagine that it is 1935 and you have $1,000 to invest. A friend urges you to buy stock on margin. Write down what you would tell your friend.

6. A chain reaction is a series of events, each one caused by the one preceding it. Explain how the crash of 1929 set off an economic chain reaction.

7. In the early 1930s, President Hoover said of the economic crisis, "We have now passed the worst…and shall rapidly recover." How might a Midwestern farmer and a member of the Bonus Army have replied to this statement?

8. What economic and natural problems did many Midwestern farmers face in the early 1930s?

9. Write a brief radio address that Herbert Hoover might have delivered to the nation in 1932 about the role of the federal government in the crisis of the Great Depression.

10. **Thinking About the Big Ideas** How did the economic changes brought on by the Great Depression threaten the nation's political system?

# CHECK-UP 5

*Answering the following questions will help you understand and remember who you have read in Chapters 19-25. Write your answers on a separate sheet of paper.*

1. The people listed below played a key role in the events of the 1930s. Tell who each person was and what she or he did to influence that decade.
   a. Franklin Roosevelt
   b. Eleanor Roosevelt
   c. Marian Anderson
   d. Frances Perkins

2. Suppose you were writing a biography of Franklin Delano Roosevelt. Why might you mention each of these places?
   a. Hyde Park
   b. Campobello
   c. Sagamore Hill

3. Define each of these terms. Then explain its relationship to FDR's political career.
   a. poliomyelitis
   b. Second Bonus Army
   c. New Deal
   d. the brain trust

4. The leadership style of FDR contrasted sharply with the style of his two predecessors—Calvin Coolidge and Herbert Hoover. Write a paragraph in which you compare these leadership styles. Use at least three of these terms in your paragraph: *optimist (optimism), exuberance, dilettante, pragmatist (pragmatism), pessimist (pessimism).*

5. What was the connection between Franklin Delano Roosevelt's family heritage and his love of history?

6. Joy Hakim states that Franklin and Eleanor Roosevelt were "one of the greatest political teams in history." What evidence supports this statement?

7. Today many people refer to handicapped people as "physically challenged" or "mentally challenged." How do you think FDR might respond to this description? Explain.

8. How did Franklin Roosevelt build upon political traditions supported by his fifth cousin Theodore Roosevelt?

9. Once in office, FDR won a new nickname—the "Happy Warrior." Do you think that name fits? Why or why not?

10. **Thinking About the Big Ideas** List some of the changes that the New Deal brought to the American political system. Then cite arguments for and against these changes. What is your opinion of the New Deal? Did it involve government too heavily in the lives of individual citizens? Explain.

# CHECK-UP 6

*Answering the following questions will help you understand and remember what you have read in Chapters 26-32. Write your answers on a separate sheet of paper.*

1. The people listed below played a key role in the events described in Chapters 26-32. Identify each person and tell what he did to increase global conflict.
    a. Adolf Hitler
    b. Francisco Franco
    c. Benito Mussolini
    d. Joseph Stalin
    e. Hideki Tojo

2. Suppose you were writing a history of the Jewish struggle against anti-Semitism. Why would you include mention of each of the following places?
    a. Egypt (in biblical times)
    b. Jerusalem (in medieval times)
    c. Cracow, Poland
    d. Oswego, New York
    e. Auschwitz, Poland
    f. Palestine (in 1942)

3. Define each of the following terms. Then explain how each term is related to the rise of Adolf Hitler.
    a. National Socialist (Nazi) Party
    b. reparations
    c. nationalism
    d. totalitarian state
    e. racism
    f. isolationism

4. In 1939, President Roosevelt delivered a blistering attack on isolation, saying:
    *There comes a time in the affairs of men when they must prepare to defend not their homes alone but the tenets [principles] of faith...upon which their churches, their governments, and their very civilization are founded.*
    What events in the world might have triggered FDR's declaration?

5. Suppose you are Liane Reif-Lehrer. Your daughter or son has just asked you why you are writing a book about your life. Compose a short dialogue in which you explain lessons that can be learned from the voyage of the *St. Louis.*

6. What was the connection between Franklin Roosevelt's love of history and the development of the atomic bomb?

7. Winston Churchill remarked:
    *War could have been prevented. The malice of the wicked was reinforced by the weakness of the virtuous.*
    What did he mean by this statement? Do you agree? Why or why not?

8. Pretend you are a reporter for your local newspaper. Write a front-page news story, complete with headline, announcing the attack on Pearl Harbor. The story should conclude with Roosevelt's war message to Congress.

9. History is full of "what ifs." For example: What if Hitler had not invaded the Soviet Union. How might the war have taken a different course?

10. **Thinking About the Big Ideas**   In a 1940 speech, Adolf Hitler summarized the developing global conflict:
    *There are two worlds that stand opposed to each other....These worlds cannot ever reconcile themselves.*
    What were the two worlds to which he referred. Do you agree or disagree? Explain.

# CHECK-UP 7

*Answering the following questions will help you understand and remember what you have read in Chapters 33-38. Write your answers on a separate sheet of paper.*

1. The people or groups listed below each played a key role in events described in Chapters 33-38. Identify each person or group and tell what each did to shape the conduct and/or outcome of World War II.
   a. Charles R. Drew
   b. John F. Kennedy
   c. Admiral Ernest King
   d. Seabees
   e. Rosie the Riveter
   f. Red Army
   g. General Dwight D. Eisenhower
   h. General Erwin Rommel
   i. General Omar Bradley

2. Suppose you were war correspondent Ernie Pyle. Why might you want to be present at each of the following sites? What headline would your write to capture the importance of events at each site?
   a. Coral Sea
   b. Midway Island
   c. Guadalcanal
   d. Omaha Beach
   e. Auschwitz
   f. Yalta
   g. Iwo Jima

3. Define each of these terms. Then explain its relationship to World War II.
   a. theater
   b. hell diver
   c. internment camp
   d. Nisei
   e. blitzkrieg
   f. front
   g. convoy
   h. bunker

4. Suppose you are President Roosevelt. It's early 1942, and you've turned over command of U.S. troops in Europe to Dwight D. Eisenhower. You've also asked Douglas MacArthur to take charge of a large force headed for the Pacific. What instructions will you give each general?

5. Imagine that you work for the National Park Service. You've been asked to design a plaque to place at the entrance of Manzanar. In 30 words or less, describe the importance of this site to U.S. history.

6. Put yourself in the shoes of one of the soldiers or nurses assigned to Guadalcanal. Write at least five diary entries describing your experiences on the island.

7. At a 1943 meeting of the Big Three, Joseph Stalin offered a toast:
   *To American production, without which this war would have been lost.*
   What do you think Stalin meant by this remark? Do you agree? Why or why not?

8. On June 12, 1944, Time magazine ran a cover story on D-Day. Time editors wrote:
   *About 15 minutes after a rosy sun lifted over the pastures of Normandy, khaki-clad U.S. and British troops began to pour ashore.*
   Pretend you are one of the editors that prepared this account. Write at least three paragraphs describing this historic landing.

9. In one paragraph, summarize the status of World War II at the end of March 1945.

10. **Thinking About the Big Ideas**   Joy Hakim says, "The unity of the Big Three did not go far beyond beating Hitler." What type of political system did each of the Big Three—Churchill, Roosevelt, and Stalin—represent? What conflicts might erupt between these systems once war ended?

# CHECK-UP 8

*Answering the following questions will help you understand and remember what you have read in Chapters 39 to 45. Write your answers on a separate sheet of paper.*

1. The people listed below played a key role in events described in Chapters 39-45. Identify each person, and tell the part he played in ending World War II.
   a. Harry Truman
   b. General Alfred Jodl
   c. Chiang Kai-shek
   d. Colonel Paul W. Tibbets, Jr.
   e. Emperor Hirohito

2. Suppose you were a cartographer, or map maker, assigned to draw a map showing key events in the closing year of World War II (1945). Why might you include each of these sites on your map?
   a. Dresden
   b. Bergen-Belsen
   c. Rheims
   d. Potsdam
   e. Hiroshima
   f. Tokyo

3. Define each of the following terms. Then explain its significance to the events of the time.
   a. Atlantic Charter
   b. self-determination
   c. strategic bombing
   d. VE Day
   e. kamikaze pilots
   f. Potsdam conference
   g. Little Boy
   h. VJ Day

4. Suppose you wanted to design a postcard to inspire U.S. troops to continue their battle against the Axis. What slogan or message might you write?

5. Put yourself in the shoes of Harry Truman. It is April 12, 1945, and you've just learned of Roosevelt's death. Confide your private thoughts about your new job as president in the form of a diary entry.

6. Write an obituary for Roosevelt that might have run in a local paper printed in Hyde Park, New York, FDR's home town.

7. Imagine you are a student in 1945. Your high school history teacher has just asked you to complete the sentence below. What will you write?
   *I'd want my children to know that World War II was a time when_____.*

8. Suppose you are Harry Truman. What arguments will you use to convince Joseph Stalin to drop demands for reparations?

9. History is filled with "what ifs." Write an answer to this one: What if the United States had not used the atomic bomb against Japan? How might the outcome of World War II have differed?

10. How did some 20th-century American artists "break the rules"? How was their work received? Give examples of specific artists and their work.

11. **Thinking About the Big Ideas**   What did World War II teach the world about totalitarianism? Do you think these lessons are still valuable for Americans in the 21st century? Why or why not?

# RESOURCE PAGE 1

Europe in 1939

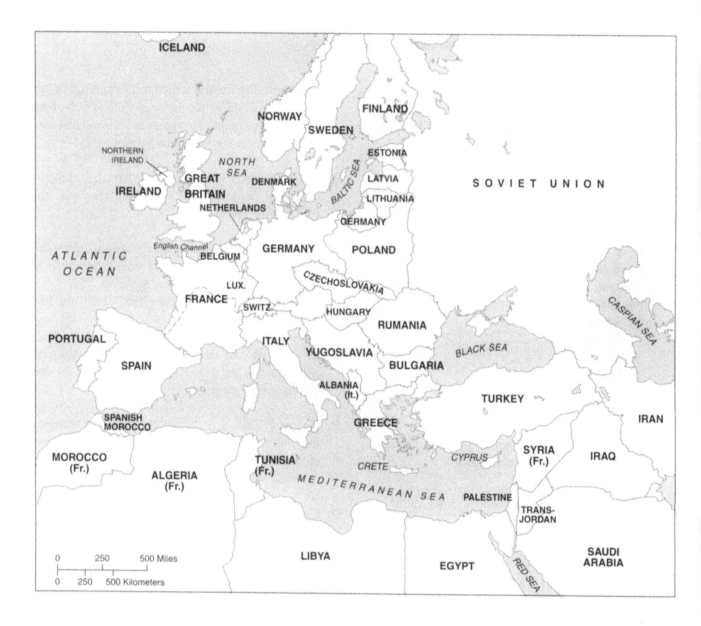

# RESOURCE PAGE 2

## Tracing the 19th Amendment's Progress

**Directions:** Study the following flowchart, and then answer the questions.

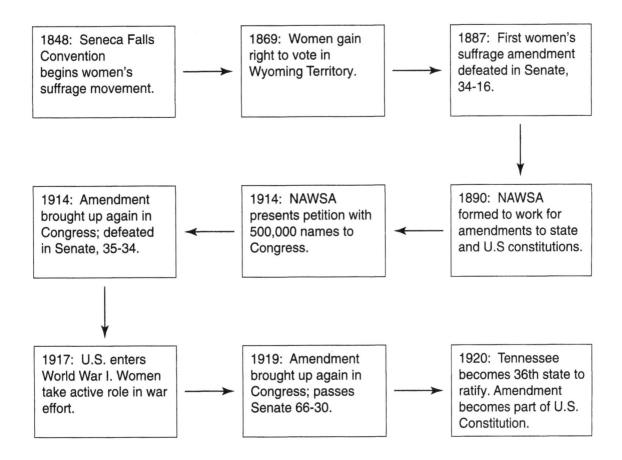

1. How many years after Seneca Falls did women win the right to vote in Wyoming? In the country as a whole?

_____

2. Describe the progress of the 19th Amendment using the votes in the Senate.

_____

_____

3. Why did the votes in the Senate change over the years?

_____

_____

4. Which event in the flowchart do you think was most important for the passage of the 19th Amendment? Why?

_____

_____

# RESOURCE PAGE 3

The United States Between the World Wars

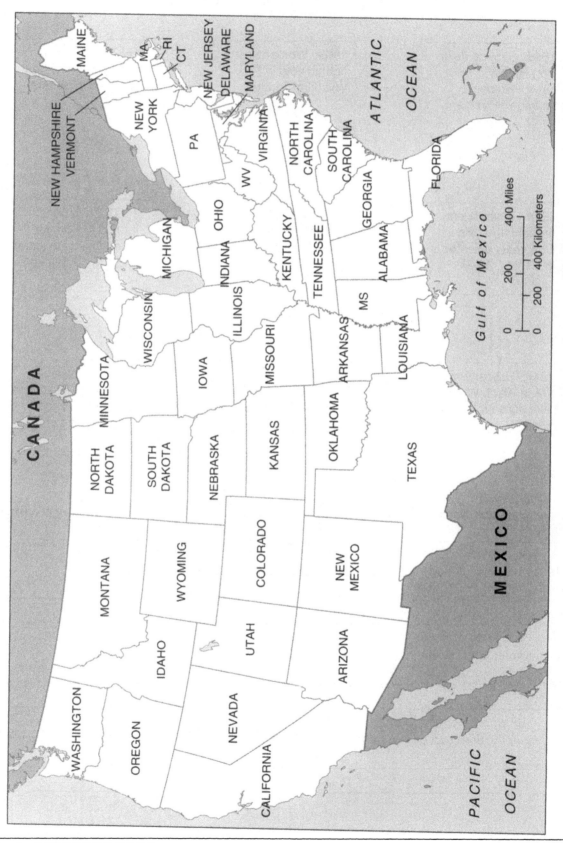

# RESOURCE PAGE 4

The World in 1939

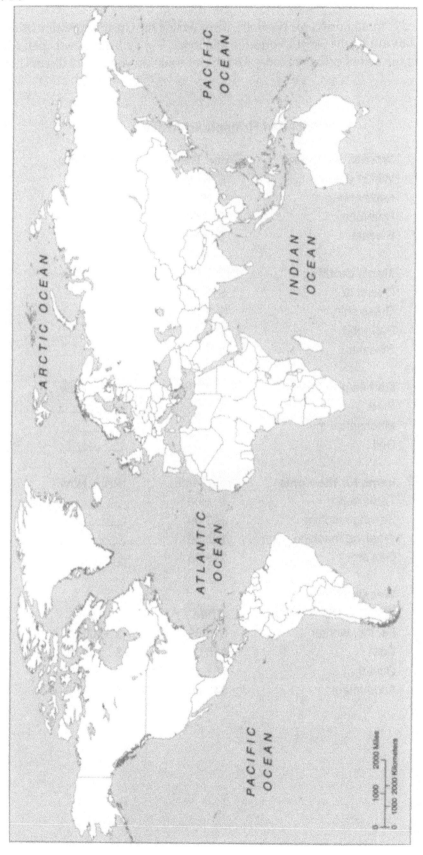

# RESOURCE PAGE 5

## Then and Now: Prices and Wages

**Directions:** Below are listed common prices for necessary items during the Great Depression. Also listed are average weekly wages for certain jobs during the Great Depression and today. Use a current newspaper, advertising circular, or store catalog to find out the cost of each item today. Use the information you find to discuss how things have changed since the 1930s.

### Prices of Household Articles

| Women's Clothing | Price Then | Price Now |
|---|---|---|
| Winter coat | $28.00 | _____ |
| Leather bag | $ 2.25 | _____ |
| Bathrobe | $ 1.00 | _____ |
| Sweater | $ 1.00 | _____ |

| Men's Clothing | Price Then | Price Now |
|---|---|---|
| Overcoat | $18.50 | _____ |
| Dress shirt | $ 1.00 | _____ |
| Bathrobe | $ 4.90 | _____ |
| Sweater | $ 1.00 | _____ |

| Games and Toys | Price Then | Price Now |
|---|---|---|
| Sled | $ 3.95 | _____ |
| Mechanical toy | $ 0.20 | _____ |
| Doll | $ 1.95 | _____ |

| Items for the Home | Price Then | Price Now |
|---|---|---|
| Table lamp | $ 1.00 | _____ |
| Sewing machine | $23.95 | _____ |
| Washing machine | $33.50 | _____ |
| Gas stove | $19.95 | _____ |

| Weekly Wages for Workers (Averages) | Then | Now |
|---|---|---|
| Factory worker | $16.89 | $ 500.00 |
| Cook | $15.00 | $ 236.00 |
| Doctor | $61.11 | $1,800.00 |
| Accountant | $45.00 | $ 700.00 |

# RESOURCE PAGE 6

## More of the New Deal's Alphabet Soup

**Directions:** Below are listed additional New Deal agencies and acts and their purposes. You can see why the federal government during the New Deal was often called an "Alphabet Soup."

| AAA | Agricultural Adjustment Act | Paid farmers to limit the production of crops and livestock |
|-----|-----|-----|
| FERA | Federal Emergency Relief Act | Gave money to local and state relief organizations |
| FLSA | Fair Labor Standards Act | Raised minimum wage to 40 cents an hour and shortened work week to 40 hours |
| FSA | Farm Security Administration | Loaned money to sharecroppers and tenant farmers so they could buy their own farms |
| HOLC | Home Owners Loan Corporation | Reduced interest on loans and provided for postponement of payments |
| NIRC | National Industry Recovery Act | Created work codes and industry safety regulations |
| NLRB | National Labor Relations Board | Guaranteed workers the right to join labor unions and call strikes |
| NRA | National Recovery Administration | Encouraged business owners and labor unions to cooperate in regulating prices, production, and wages |

# RESOURCE PAGE 7

The Pacific Theater of War

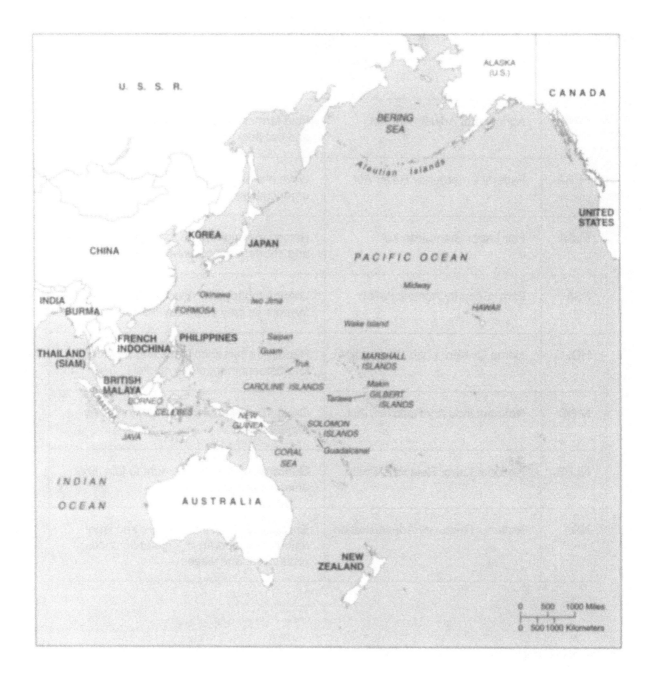

# RESOURCE PAGE 8

## Analyzing a Photograph

Directions: Follow your teacher's instructions to use this page.

### Observation

1. Describe the people in the photograph.

_____

_____

2. Describe the setting of the photograph.

_____

_____

3. Describe the activities in the photograph.

_____

_____

### Interpretation

4. Based on your observations, what are three things you might infer from this photograph?

_____

_____

5. Why was this photograph taken?

_____

_____

. Who might have taken this photograph?

_____

_____

### Evaluation

7. What questions does this photograph raise in your mind?

_____

_____

8. What new ideas about history have you learned from this photograph?

_____

_____

# ANSWER KEY

## CHECK-UP 1

1. (a) U.S. president during World War I (b) France's prime minister who wanted reparations from Germany (c) Supreme Court justice who stated "clear and present danger" policy (d) educator who criticized U.S. medical education

2. The League of Nations was part of the peace treaty presented at Versailles. That treaty was not ratified by the U.S. Senate in Washington largely because of the provisions for a League of Nations.

3. (a) not taking sides (b) the right of people to choose their own form of government (c) staying out of foreign affairs (d) spying (e) inciting others to rebel (f) disease that spreads across many nations

4. advance the cause of democracy in the world

5. (a) The United States might not have entered the war when it did or might never have entered the war. (b) The invitation might have reduced Republican opposition to the treaty.

6. While Wilson wanted a lasting peace and a new world order, the Big Four nations wanted revenge.

7. Students' choices and reasons will vary.

8. While the influenza epidemic took more lives, the war changed the way the nation thought and lived.

9. Answers should indicate that prewar conditions for the soldier were far better than for a sharecropper or sweatshop worker and he would be most likely to favor a return to former conditions.

10. Students should cite Republican opposition to the peace treaty.

## CHECK-UP 2

1. (a) Both were suffragists working for passage of the 19th Amendment. (b) Bryan was prosecutor and Darrow was defense attorney in the Scopes "monkey" trial.

2. (a) town where women took over government when all the women voted and many men didn't (b) naval oil reserve near Casper, Wyoming, involved in a Harding-era scandal; (c) section of New York City with large African American population that created the Harlem Renaissance (d) site of the Scopes "monkey" trial on teaching evolution in Tennessee public schools

3. (a) outlawing all drinking of alcohol (b) person who worked for women's right to vote (c) person who sold alcohol illegally (d) person who doesn't believe in any government (e) young woman during the Jazz Age who wore short hair, short skirts, and lipstick

4. It was noble because it tried to make people do something that lawmakers thought was good for them. Opinions will vary on whether it deserved that label.

5. Letters should state that suffragists want Wilson to use his influence to win passage of an amendment giving women the right to vote.

6. Memoranda should say that Palmer fears the spread of communism and anarchism and that foreigners suspected of communism or anarchy should be rounded up, jailed, and deported.

7. Evidence in the chapter indicates that most voters were becoming aware of Harding's lack of qualifications and corruption in his government.

8. Students should note that not all Americans shared in the prosperity and that some suffered abridgement of their rights.

9. Both measures required Constitutional Amendments; and women were the greatest supporters of both measures.

10. Students should discuss the Red Scare, the arrest of suffragists at the White House, and the Scopes trial in their answers.

## CHECK-UP 3

1. (a) player who made baseball a hitters' game and set home run records (b) woman who was outstanding in many sports and was voted best woman athlete of the first half of the 20th century (c) African American track star who took four gold medals at the 1936 Olympics (d) trumpet player and one of the greatest jazz musicians (e) pianist and composer, another of the greatest jazz musicians (f) scientist considered the father of rocket science (g) first to fly a plane solo across the Atlantic Ocean

2. New Orleans was the cradle of jazz. Hollywood became the capital of U.S. movie-making

3. (a) left-handed person (b) tour with a baseball team or to give airplane shows (c) unique American music that probably began in New Orleans (d) doing your own thing with music (e) device propelled into the air or into space

4. Inscriptions should note Ruth's hitting prowess and his role in changing baseball.

5. Advertisements might draw on names and quotations from the chapter.

6. Possible answer: Jazz arose from a combination of cultures unique to the United States.

7. Letters might indicate that Goddard's inventions could open a new frontier—space—to Americans.

8. Cartoons will vary.

9. Answers might cite publicity over sports figures; others might say that Lindbergh received too much publicity for a flight that was bound to happen.

10. Possible answers: Ruth for changing baseball from a defensive to an offensive game; Armstrong for popularizing jazz; Goddard for laying the groundwork for the space age.

## CHECK-UP 4

1. (a) ran unsuccessfully for president against Hoover in 1928 (b) became president in 1929 and served during onset of Great Depression, which he kept saying was ending (c) general whose troops attacked the Bonus Army (d) became President in 1933 and began programs to get the nation back to work

2. (a) financial center that was the location of the stock market boom and bust in the 1920s (b) location of the White House, where the Bonus Army went to ask President Hoover for help (c) location of the Dust Bowl farms that were devastated by drought during the Depression

3. (a) share of ownership in a company (b) idea that prices increase when there is not enough of something and decrease when there is too much of something (c) time when stock prices are rising (d) time of wild selling of stocks that nobody will buy (e) time of decline in business activity along with falling prices and high unemployment (f) Depression-era shanty town made of boxes and boards (g) thrown out of your home (h) individuals helping one another

4. Answers should note the anti-urban feeling that grew as the nation moved away from its rural past, and helped Hoover win the election.

5. Answers should express wariness about buying on margin after the experience of Black Thursday in 1929.

6. Possible answer: Losses incurred by buying stock on margin led to inability to pay mortgages, which led to loss of homes, which led to banks not receiving mortgage payments and then failing.

7. Both farmers and members of the Bonus Army would cite continuing problems as evidence that the worst was not over.

8. Farmers faced economic problems from overproduction and falling crop prices. They also faced years of drought and other natural disasters. Both problems led to the loss of farms.

9. Radio addresses might note a willingness to grant some federal aid to big businesses but should stress that individual citizens should help one another.

10. Possible answer: When it appeared that the U.S. government was not willing or able to cope with the economic crisis, some citizens began to favor following other political systems, such as communism, which seemed to be coping better with economic problems.

# CHECK-UP 5

1. (a) president from 1933 who began New Deal to help people suffering from the Great Depression (b) president's wife who changed the role of First Lady by being the link to the people (c) famous black singer who was refused use of a concert hall in Washington, and who Eleanor Roosevelt encouraged to sing at the Lincoln Memorial (d) secretary of labor and first woman cabinet member

2. (a) where FDR grew up (b) FDR's summer home in New Brunswick, Canada (c) home of Theodore Roosevelt, which Franklin visited as a child

3. (a) crippling disease that almost forced FDR from politics; overcoming it made him a better leader (b) FDR offered the Second Bonus Army use of an army camp, food and coffee, doctors, a navy band to play, and sent his wife to visit (c) FDR's program to get the country back to work (d) FDR's advisors, many of whom were college professors

4. Paragraphs might suggest that FDR's *optimism* contrasted sharply with the ineffectiveness of Coolidge and Hoover, that FDR's *exuberant* attitude kept people hopeful, that FDR was no longer a *dilettante* but a man with a goal, that FDR's *pragmatism* made him willing to try many solutions and keep those that worked, and that *pessimism* was not part of FDR's public persona.

5. FDR's family was connected to U.S. history and he became involved in the combined history of family and nation.

6. Answers should focus on the role that Eleanor played as FDR's "legs, eyes, and ears" as well as her individual political activities that set her apart from most earlier First Ladies.

7. Students might indicate FDR's tendency to view problems as challenges and his refusal to live life as an invalid.

8. FDR built on Progressive ideals popular at the end of the 19th century and the beginning of the 20th century, the period when Theodore Roosevelt was most active.

9. Students might cite FDR's sense of optimism and his belief in action.

10. *Changes:* Increased power of the executive and involvement of the federal government in the economy and in the lives of individuals. *Pro arguments:* prevented the collapse of capitalism and democracy, helped relieve economic suffering, reduced gaps between rich and poor. *Con arguments:* increased size of national debt, increased taxes, undermined free enterprise. Student opinions will vary.

# CHECK-UP 6

1. (a) German dictator who began invading other countries and attacking Jews and other people (b) Spanish dictator (c) Italian dictator who sent troops into Ethiopia and allied with Hitler (d) Soviet communist dictator who killed many Soviet people (e) Japanese military dictator who invaded China and tortured and killed many Chinese civilians

2. (a) Jews were enslaved in Egypt. (b) During the Crusades, Christians murdered Jews in Jerusalem. (c) Jews from Cracow were sent to concentration camps where many were murdered. (d) Jewish immigrants to the U.S. who were denied visas were interned at a camp in Oswego. (e) Auschwitz was a concentration camp where many Jews were starved and murdered. (e) Although the League of Nations gave Jews the right to buy land in Palestine, the British pressured other countries to refuse to let them emigrate.

3. (a) Hitler led the Nazi Party, which pushed him into the dictatorship. (b) Hitler used the anger at reparations after World War I to fuel German anger about the Treaty of Versailles. (c) Hitler's brand of nationalism was a belief that love of one's country is more important than anything else, including truth. (d) Hitler ran a totalitarian state in which only the state is important, with no regard for the individual. (e) Hitler based his racism on pseudo-science and said races should keep their blood pure by getting rid of problems and non-Aryans. (f)

Isolationist pressure kept the United States from getting involved and thus allowed Hitler to flourish unopposed.

4. Students might cite terrible aggression, suppression of human rights under totalitarianism, Nazi persecution of people on the basis of religion and race.

5. Dialogues should highlight Joy Hakim's remarks about the United States giving sanction to bigots.

6. Sachs got Roosevelt's attention by citing Napoleon's fateful decision not to listen to Robert Fulton. Roosevelt decided not to repeat this error.

7. Aggressors took advantage of isolationism by rearming and picking off nations one by one. The "virtuous" had allowed this wickedness to continue unchallenged.

8. News stories should reflect the information about the time and place of Japan's attack. Students should use facts from pages 129-131 to answer a reporter's questions—*Who? What? When? Where? Why? How?*

9. Some students might say that England and the United States would have won the war but with far greater loss of life. Others may believe that Hitler's forces would have been able to hang onto western Europe. Still others may believe that it was inevitable that Hitler and Stalin—two ambitious dictators—would eventually clash.

10. Hitler referred to the democratic world and the totalitarian world. Most students will agree that these two systems are incompatible. One system is based upon protecting individual rights; the other is based on strengthening the state at the expense of the individual.

# CHECK-UP 7

1. (a) developed the idea for a blood bank, which saved many lives in World War II (b) commanded a PT boat that was rammed by a Japanese destroyer; heroically helped save himself and other survivors (c) urged that the United States go on the offensive against the Japanese in the Pacific (d) construction crews that repaired airfields and equipment (e) symbol of can-do for women who took over jobs usually done by men (f) trapped a German army at Stalingrad and then went on the offensive against Germany (g) successfully led the war against Germany's Afrika Korps and the D-Day invasion (h) German "desert fox" who led his troops to early victories in Africa, but was eventually defeated by combined Allied attacks (i) led D-Day landings

2. Headlines should suggest: (a) The Coral Sea was a 1942 battle from which the Japanese had to retreat. (b) The ferocious battle at Midway Island proved the importance of air power in a hard-won American victory. (c) Guadalcanal posed enormous problems, but the U.S. victory was a turning point in the war in the Pacific. (d) Omaha Beach was a site in the U.S. part of the D-Day invasion of German-held France. (e) Allied liberators find skeletal-like inmates and evidence of 3 million people murdered at Auschwitz. (f) Churchill, Roosevelt, and Stalin met at Yalta to plan the final battles and agree on establishing the United Nations. (e) When American GIs captured Iwo Jima, they raised a flag on top of Mr. Suribachi.

3. (a) area of activity in which troops fought; Pacific theater or Western theater (b) U.S. Navy bombers who sank many Japanese ships (c) camps in remote locations where Japanese Americans were sent (d) American citizens who were children of Japanese immigrants (e) "lightning war," German mechanized attacks featuring fast advances led by aircraft and tanks (f) a battle line; Americans fought on a Pacific front and a European front. Russia's front with Germany was known as the Eastern front. (g) groups of troop or supply ships traveling together with destroyers for protection. (h) building made of thick concrete designed to shield heavy guns from attack

4. Possible answer: FDR might order Eisenhower to give unseasoned troops experience in North Africa and then devise a plan for invading Europe. He might tell MacArthur to take back the Philippines.

5. Plaques should get across the idea that Manzanar stands as a symbol

of injustice suffered when the Constitution is sidestepped for racial reasons.

6. Diary entries should reflect descriptions and events in Chapter 35. Details may include the island's beauty, its heat, dangerous animals, jungle, mud, kunai grass, tough battles for Henderson Field, SNAFUs, losses of people, tropical diseases, sea fights, Seabees at work, and so on.

7. He meant that U.S. factories supplied the weapons, supplies, etc., to keep armies in the field. Most students will agree. They might cite the near collapse of the Allies in 1942, before the United States became fully in wartime production.

8. Paragraphs should reflect the details in Chapter 37, including lives lost, difficulties getting on shore, enemy mines and bunkers, code names of the beaches, eventual Allied triumph.

9. Paragraphs should comment on the last-ditch stand of the Axis.

10. Churchill and Roosevelt represented democratic systems; Stalin represented a totalitarian system. *Possible conflicts:* territorial control, punishment of Germany, governments set up in Allied-occupied territory, and so on.


## CHECK-UP 8

1. (a) became president after FDR's death; made fateful decision to drop atomic bomb; negotiated peace treaties (b) signed the German surrender (c) China's leader; called for Japan's unconditional surrender (d) flew the *Enola Gay*, which dropped the atomic bomb on Hiroshima (e) Japanese emperor who overruled Japanese warlords and surrendered

2. (a) German city destroyed by heavy Allied fire bombing (b) concentration camp where Anne Frank died (c) place where Germans signed surrender documents (d) conference where Stalin demanded huge reparations, but where Truman and Churchill refused and threatened to leave (e) Japanese city destroyed by first atomic bomb (f) where Japanese army officers broke into emperor's palace after Emperor Hirohito's surrender to try to stop his radio broadcast

3. (a) document signed by Roosevelt and Churchill stating that after the war nations would choose their own forms of government (b) the right of nations to choose their own forms of government and not be taken over by imperialist powers (c) the bombing of cities, intended to force surrender; often toughened people's will to fight back. (d) May 8, 1945, marked Victory in Europe (e) Japanese pilots trained for suicide missions (f) meeting of Truman, Churchill, Stalin, and Chiang Kai-shek to plan the end of the war (g) name given to the atomic bomb dropped on Hiroshima (h) August 15, 1945, the date of Victory in Japan

4. Possible messages might include any ideals for which Americans fought—democracy, liberty, justice. They might also include slogans that oppose totalitarianism.

5. Diary entries might include a sense of the suddenness of the event, the weight of the office, the difficulty of following FDR, and the determination to do the best for the country.

6. Obituaries should include FDR's life in Hyde Park, his family connections, and his accomplishments as president.

7. Students should think in terms of U.S. war goals and the efforts of its military and civilian people.

8. Answers should focus on the role reparations played in fueling the rise of Adolf Hitler and Germany's buildup to World War II.

9. Some students might point to high casualties on both sides that conventional warfare would have produced. Others might say that the war could have dragged on for years at a stalemate. Still others might say that the world might not have entered the atomic age.

10. They painted pictures from real life, or street scenes and working people. The art establishment wanted nothing to do with them. Examples may be taken from works reproduced in Book Nine or from other works students might know.

11. Answers will vary.


## RESOURCE PAGE 1

Students' maps should include the major events and battles in the European theater of war.


## RESOURCE PAGE 2

1. 72 years

2. The first vote in 1887 was lopsidedly against it. The second vote, in 1914, was close, but not the two-thirds majority needed. In the third vote, in 1919, the amendment won the two-thirds majority needed.

3. Suffragists and their supporters brought more and more pressure on Congress. Women proved by their activities in World War I that they deserved the right to full participation in society.

4. Possible answer: Women's activity during World War I, because after that they could not be denied the right to vote.


## RESOURCE PAGE 3

Students' maps should include important sites in the United States mentioned in the text.


## RESOURCE PAGE 4

Students' maps should include important sites in the world mentioned in the text.


## RESOURCE PAGE 5

This resource page is to be used with the Student Team Learning Activity in Part 4.


## RESOURCE PAGE 6

This resource page is to be used with the Student Team Learning Activity in Part 5.


## RESOURCE PAGE 7

Students' maps should include the major events and battles in the Pacific theater of war.


## RESOURCE PAGE 8

This Resource Page is to be used with the Student Team Learning Activity in Part 6.

9 780199 767434